LEGAL STRATEGY

LEGAL STRATEGY

PAUL J. ZWIER

NATIONAL INSTITUTE FOR TRIAL ADVOCACY

Reproduction Permission
National Institute for Trial Advocacy
53550 Generations Drive
South Bend, IN 46635

(800) 225-6482
E-mail: nita.1@nd.edu

Fax (574) 271-8375
Web site: www.nita.org

Zwier, Paul J., *Legal Strategy* (NITA, 2005).

ISBN 1-55681-923-4

Library of Congress Cataloging-in-Publication Data

Zwier, Paul J., 1954-

SUMMARY OF CONTENTS

CONTENTS

ACKNOWLEDGMENTS

This book is a product of the accumulated wisdom of a number of great trial lawyers and teachers that I have worked with during my twenty-plus years with NITA.

Of special mention is Deanne C. Siemer, who first introduced me to the idea of describing the pretrial litigation process in terms of legal strategy, created a case file designed to teach it, and greatly assisted me with insights about the practice of strategic decision making and with a careful and detailed edit of an early draft of this book. In particular, her "principled" approach to planning for an giving legal advice is transformative in that it shows the lawyer how to be practical and ethical at the same time. Frank D. Rothschild needs special thanks, for his ideas permeate my understanding of how to put a case together, including how to think about a case as an important visual tool for teaching a client, opponent, mediator, and court about the strengths and weaknesses of the case.

And finally, I must make special mention of Anthony J. Bocchino, who has contributed enormously to my understanding of the pretrial litigation process. His ideas and insights from my first days of teaching and lawyering, and his contributions to a coauthored NITA book on fact investigation continue to be integral to my understanding of legal strategy in a litigation setting. My research assistant, Michelle Marks, provided invaluable research and editing help.

INTRODUCTION

Today's litigators need to be able to think strategically. Not only must they understand how to put a case together for trial, they also need to understand the clients' business and long term goals in order to be able give their clients wise advice. They need to be able to determine where the client wants to go and how best to get there. They need to be able to get information (both facts and feelings) from the client as well give clear, precise, comprehensive advice to the client. To that end they need to be skilled interviewers, brainstormers, fact investigation planners, and comprehensive thinkers, as well as informed, strategic thinkers, wise counselors, and negotiators.

Once a lawyer accurately determines where the client wants to go—the ends he desires—then the process requires reverse engineering from the end goals back to the facts and procedural alternatives most likely to get there. Sometimes this means the client should just walk away from the dispute, because litigating will distract the client from getting where the client needs to go. Sometimes it will mean that the lawyer will teach the client how to resolve the client's dispute for him or herself. Sometimes there is persuasion involved, where the lawyer may persuade the officer of an institutional client why the firm is better off taking a particular approach to resolving the dispute. Sometimes, where the dispute concerns matters of principle or where the client needs to establish a legal precedent, then a trial might be the best course. Legal strategy helps the lawyer discern when to advise the client to play his litigation cards, or when to "hold em, or when to walk away, or even, when to run."

As used here, legal strategy is the "skills" part of legal judgment or wisdom. These skills are not sufficient in and of themselves. After all, the foundation for the qualities necessary to the lawyer's craft lie in character traits and deep knowledge that one would not characterize as "skills" at all—personal integrity, an inner moral compass, and a perception of one's work as embedded in broad social, economic, political, historical, and for some, spiritual contexts. Still, while judgment is an ensemble of settled dispositions, broad judgment and quick intelligence, a focus on skills can start to teach judgment by focusing lawyers in a continual exercise in deliberation on what matters most.

That is what these materials seek to do. And their focus is on the legal process pre-litigation, transactional, and negotiation process, and those processes that are alongside litigation. With respect to litigation these processes focus both on whether to litigate and determine whether to choose alternative strategies to the traditional litigation process. Legal strategy in the context of pre-litigation, or alongside litigation, is the process that brings together skills from a range of disciplines. Each of the disciplines has a substantial literature of its own. In this book, the process is described in a way that brings together the basics of each discipline and provides references for further reading in depth on each skill.

Some argue that professional (client-centered) strategic decision making is strategic decision making, especially when it involves a professional and a client; whether for architect, engineer, doctor, or lawyer. It involves three basic steps: gathering facts and defining the problem, counseling the client for the client's input and consent for what steps will be taken on the client's behalf, and the implementation of the client's decision. The steps in legal strategy can be defined more particularly as follows:

◂▪▸**Step 1—fact investigation and issue formulation.** The lawyer needs to define the problem or decision.

◂▪▸**Step 2—client counseling.** The lawyer needs to identify the client's (or other relevant parties') goals, underlying objectives, assign priorities or weights to those objectives, and specify the criteria in terms of which solution will be evaluated. For the counseling to be effective for the client, the lawyer needs to be able to generate alternative solutions or courses of action and then assess the alternatives. The lawyer needs to help the client evaluate the consequences of each alternative according to how well they satisfy the client's underlying objectives. As a part of this counseling process the lawyer must update and go deeper in gathering client-centered information (understanding client values, risk preferences, social and psychological makeup, and particular economic concerns) necessary to assess each alternative to help the client select the optimal course of action according to the expected effectiveness in meeting underlying goals. In this regard the lawyer needs to present advice in a way that both respects client autonomy and calls the client with wisdom to its higher and best self.

◆■▶ Step 3—implementation of the client's decision through the right dispute resolution process, either negotiation, mediation, or adjudication. The lawyer needs to think strategically about each dispute resolution process, to best implement the client's decision and monitor its implementation, being prepared to re-engage in the decision-making process as unforeseen problems are encountered.

Devising a legal strategy is a task that is readily defined:

How do we get from "here" to "there" within the existing constraints of time and money?

To be successful at legal strategy, a lawyer needs to define "here" accurately and efficiently. In other words, the lawyer needs to know the limitations that operate in the real world, and that constrict a possible more theoretical and complicated decision analysis.

What are the facts about the situation as it exists today? What level of certainty (probabilities) that the facts are as the client sees them? What facts or policies lie below the horizon, but are non the less operating? The existing constraints of time and money may change as events unfold, but it is important to define them accurately so that the strategy fits the problem.

Next, the lawyer needs to help the client to define "there" in a practical fashion. What alternatives best serve the client's goals and interests? What consequences—economic, social, legal, and moral—are likely with each alternative?

What is an acceptable outcome? Skillful lawyers usually focus on an acceptable outcome rather than a "good" outcome or a "total win" outcome in order to have more flexibility in devising a strategy.

This book is organized chronologically.

> **Chapter 1 will discuss Step 1, and explore the process of defining the problem and framing the issue for the client, and the skills necessary to do this.** It will focus on document management, client interviewing, and witness interviewing as key skills in best defining the problem for the client.

> **Chapter 2 will also deal with Step 1, as it will describe techniques for finding facts in addition to those facts that come from the clients**: including documents from opponents, third persons, and interviews with unfriendly witnesses.

> **Chapter 3 will deal with case analysis, including: defining the client's problem**—how to develop the best legal theories, factual theories, and themes for the case. It will frame the "deep issue" in the case as a way of not only helping the client understand the situation, but as an important step in strategizing about how to solve the problem.

> **Chapter 4 focuses on the counseling process.** It will show how to prepare the client for the decisions to be made by developing the key alternative solutions, and gathering information that will help the client judge the likely consequences of each alternative. This chapter will explore decision making frameworks grounded in the rules of professional responsibility and three alternative models taken from moral philosophy and ethics to help propose

a fourth practical and integrated approach to counseling and legal strategy.

Chapter 5 will focus on how best to strategize to implement the client's decisions by testing the strategy through negotiation and mediation. It will take the lawyer through strategic models useful for preparing to negotiate or work with a mediator to design a solution that fits the client's goals. Of course, if these efforts fail, then the lawyer has also best positioned the case for its resolution in court. In other words, chapter 5 will show the lawyer how to make best strategic use of the pretrial process for a resolution most consistent with the client's goals.

⟨•⟩ ⟨•⟩ ⟨•⟩

Homestead Properties Inc.
A Legal Strategy Case File

To keep our discussion from spinning off into abstract theory, this book will make use of a NITA case file for examples. The case file is called *Homestead Properties Inc., A Legal Strategy Case File*, and deals with Homestead, a construction company that mass manufactures low-cost, prefabricated individual housing units for apartment developments in Georgia and Florida. The business was started by the Steadman brothers in the early 1990s and incorporated in Nita City in 1999.

All of the apartment complexes constructed by Homestead were identical in design and construction. The only difference was the number of units in each complex. They were all modular construction consisting of factory-built 12' x 24' sections that were transported to the site and arranged side-by-side and back-to-back on concrete block foundations. Usually there is a stem wall in the front and support piers in the back, which allows a crawl space under each unit.

Homestead's Chief Financial Officer Eleanor Addington is a young a fast rising officer in the company, who started with the company when it was still a family operation. In the case file as it rolls out, Ms. Addington comes to the company's lawyer with three different problems. The first concerns a problem with a competitor, Best Homes, who seems to be engaged in a campaign of product disparagement of Homestead's properties, telling prospective buyers that Homestead's homes are poorly made and termite infested. The second part concerns a discovery by Homestead that their properties are indeed, termite infested, and the company's claim under its insurance policy with American Insurance Company, for coverage of the problem. The third part deals with Homestead Properties claims under its excess policy carrier, Manhattan Casualty company, for its claims of termite damage in excess of the $25 million cap on its policy with American.

This last situation between Homestead Properties and Manhattan will be the focus of much of our examples in the following chapters. It involves the interpretation of an insurance contract, and questions of parole evidence from a meeting Homestead's CFO Eleanor Addington had with a Mr. Alex Hirp (an insurance broker), and David Cosham (representing Manhattan Insurance, recently deceased). There are some notes that have been recovered of the meeting, but the notes are subject to different interpretations of what happened. So the situation presents classic reconstruction problems and is subject to different narratives, depending on what side of the case the teller of the narrative is on. It provides of excellent paradigm for discussing legal strategy.

Further Reading

Books

Deanne C. Siemer *Teacher's Manual, Homestead Properties, Inc. Case File* (NITA, ___).

Anthony Kronman, *The Lost Lawyer: Failing Ideals in the Legal Profession* (Harvard Press, 1993).

Articles

See, Paul Brest, Linda Krieger, Charles T. Munger, *Symposium on 21st Century Lawyer: on Teaching Professional Judgment*, 69 Wash. L. Rev. 527, (1994)

CHAPTER ONE
CLIENT FACTS AS THE FOUNDATION
FOR A LEGAL STRATEGY

Facts speak louder than eloquence.—Chinese Proverb

Facts are generally overesteemed. For most practical purposes, a thing is what men think it is.—John Updike (b. 1912) U. S. author, critic. The Statesman Buchanan, in *Buchanan, Dying*: act 1 (1974).

Strategic fact investigation gets to the important facts quickly so that the initial assessments about alternative courses of action can be made promptly, before the situation gets worse. This kind of fact investigation takes advantage of routine business practices to digitize data and documents—evidence of wrongdoing or lack of wrongdoing—and the capabilities to search this data so that the potential parties in a lawsuit can better determine their own responsibility in bringing about the dispute. The Federal Rules of Civil Procedure in fact contemplate these technological advances. The rules contemplate quick, voluntary disclosure. They provide the incentive to self investigate to determine whether to fight and how to fight. In addition, the lawyer must identify and design a strategy for interviewing the client and client employees.

1.1 Client Documents

In any serious matter, it is useful to have a preliminary look at documents as early in the process as possible. In business or commercial matters, witnesses may become locked into perceptions or theories that cannot work given the content of available documents. Although it is widely known by judges and juries that people sometimes write documents for self-protection, rather than to accurately record the facts, most relevant documents get serious consideration in any form of dispute resolution.

1.1.1 E-mail

When individuals are involved in non-business disputes, e-mails may not have been saved with regularity. However, in business situations, all e-mails are usually saved for some time period. Archived e-mails are easy to search, and usually turn up informal views on the subject of the dispute. For example, the CEO may tell the lawyer that the product is solid, has never had any problems, and that the employees think it is just grand. An electronic search of the company's e-mail will quickly reveal what employees think of the product, what kinds of problems have gotten attention within the company, and how specific problems with the product have been addressed. This kind of electronic search is inexpensive and relatively quick. The lawyer provides the search terms that define the general area of the problem, and those search terms are run, using standard search software, against the digital archives of company e-mails for the relevant period of time. The "hits" are ranked for relevance by the search software, and browsing the highly ranked hits will give the lawyer a quick overview of how the company has dealt with the problem.

1.1.2 Technology and "The Smoking Gun"

Similarly, it is important in any serious dispute to capture the most relevant documents in digital format as quickly as possible so that they can be searched for potential "smoking gun" material. If it is highly likely that there is no smoking gun document, then the strategist may have greater flexibility in developing workable case theories. Technology makes it relatively easy to capture the content of a lot of documents in short order. For example, if a company has a problem with an employee who has not been promoted and who threatens to sue, it would be useful to the strategist to know very early on what the documentary record looks like. This can be done by bringing a portable document scanner to the department where the employee works, and scanning all of the files of the employee's supervisor.

Once the files are scanned, they are turned into digitally "readable" format with optical character recognition software, a very speedy process. These files can then be searched for adverse comments about the employees, adverse comments about the projects on which the employees worked, or positive assessments of either. The files of the immediate supervisor are not the only place that relevant documents might be located in a case like this, but these are the files most likely to contain a smoking gun document. All of the locations where possibly relevant documents might be located can be searched as the fact investigation proceeds, but it is important to strike quickly where the most important documents are likely to be. Competent litigation support personnel can scan 20,000 to 40,000 pages a day, depending on the nature of the material. Optical character recognition (OCR) processing takes a few seconds a page, depending on the speed and capacity of the computer equipment. In most cases, lawyers can have a searchable database of 20,000 to 40,000 pages within a few days.

Because lawyer and paralegal time is expensive, it is inefficient to have people reading documents before software has located the subset of the documents most likely to contain the needed information. The cost of scanning core documents up front is much less than the cost of handling paper copies of documents many times over as inevitably happens in disputed matters. Commercial scanning is about 15 cents a page, and commercial OCR processing is another 5 cents to 10 cents a page. Lawyers can outsource the storage of and access to collections of digital files to document repositories for quite reasonable fees. The document repository service provider includes the document management and search capabilities as a part of the service.

1.1.2.1 **Internet Searches**

The internet may also yield useful information very early in the fact investigation process. Searches result using each of the five principal search engines (Google, Yahoo, Microsoft engines, etc.) should be examined to determine whether employees or others have posted information that needs to be considered.

1.2 **Client Interviews**

You should not think of interviewing as a generic skill. Interviewing clients takes a different skill than interviewing neutral witnesses, interested witnesses, or hostile witnesses. The appropriate interviewing model depends on the eagerness of the interviewee to talk. The interviewing techniques will differ from the situation where the interviewee does not trust the lawyer and does not see it in his best interest to talk. The following model assumes a basic willingness on the part of the interviewee to talk, and uses the client as an example. It expects that the client has thought out or is in the process of thinking out their problem and its legal implications, and is willing to trust the lawyer with a full description of the problem. The following model also assumes a client-centered approach to information gathering in which the lawyer is viewed as a professional, capable and desirous of, first and foremost serving the client's interests. Finally, this model assumes that the lawyer subverts their self interest to the interests and goals of the client

1.2.1 **Goals of The Client Versus Goals of The Lawyer**

CLIENT GOALS	LAWYER GOALS
To get and give information that can solve their problem	To get legally relevant information that is "valid," complete, and accurate
To get reassurance	To get information that is likely to lead to other relevant information
To get empathy and an empathetic ear	To develop rapport
To get recognition	To begin to evaluate the client as a possible witness
Catharsis	
Assess the lawyer	
Determine cost	

1.2.2 **Conflicting Motivations**

A number of goals are in conflict here. The reassurance and sympathy (as opposed to empathy) needed by the client may not be the lawyer's to give. Cost may also get in the way of the client's giving complete information. The lawyer's need to evaluate the client's case may also block the information exchange. These goal conflicts create competing motivations, which can be described as inhibitors and facilitators.

Inhibitors include:

Ego threat	The client withholds information that threatens self esteem
Case threat	The client withholds information that threatens their view of the case and its result
Role expectations	The client may expect that the lawyer will take control and do the questioning and may be too quiet
Etiquette barrier	The client and lawyer may think that there are things one does not talk about information related to personal finances, religion, politics, or sexual conduct
Trauma	The client may resist thinking about unpleasant memories such as anger, bad conduct, injury, or embarrassment
Perceived irrelevance	The client may feel there is no need to provide this detailed information
Greater need	The client may be unwilling or unable to attend to the lawyer's question because he feels there is something more important that the lawyer needs to know that the lawyer hasn't asked about, or that the client has avoided saying
Forgetting	Memories fade, people perceive things differently[1]
Chronological confusion	The client recalls events but is unsure of sequence
Inferential confusion	The client is desirous of a certain result and infers facts from the desire; he knows the employee is honest so he infers the client would have told him if something went wrong, and therefore must have told him all was going well—the confusion could either be from induction or deduction

---

1. See §2.5 on memory.

In order to counteract these inhibitors the lawyer must use certain facilitators. More will be said about these in the section on **Witness Interviewing.**

Facilitators include:	
Empathetic understanding	Including various probes and active listening skills[2]
Fulfilling expectations	Lawyer may say, "I understand how hard it is to recall; I've often had that difficulty myself. Often I find, however, that if I concentrate for awhile, and try to put myself back in time and place, things start to come back. So take your time and think a little more" (Use memory flood)
Recognition	Lawyer may say, "You're doing a good job" or "That's important—what you have said so far"
Extrinsic rewards	Where appropriate, the lawyer might say, "This information will be helpful in avoiding liability"
Catharsis	Where the lawyer determines that the client is inhibited by strongly held emotions, the lawyer might try to release them by encouraging their expression, in order that the witness can put them behind him and give more detail
Need for meaning	The lawyer might create cognitive dissonance by raising conflicting information, in order to spur the client into giving more information. If the lawyer uses this technique he should raise the conflict as coming from the opposition, or the jury, or the judge, rather than from the lawyer, in order to protect the client from a feeling that the lawyer is not on the client's side. The lawyer might say, "You know a judge might be curious about this letter? Does it not indicate you knew at the time you renewed the insurance that you had a problem? How would we answer the judge's concern?"

---

2. *See* section 1.3.1 on probes.

1.2.3 **An Overall Client Interview Strategy**

The following interview model is offered so the lawyer can start to control behavior and make choices about what he does and asks about, rather than to simply react. Skills learning models are not meant to be cookbook tricks for successful client relationships, but are meant to allow the lawyer to ask questions, not because he can't think of anything else to say, but because he has a reason for asking a question.

1.2.3.1 **A "Bucket Bailer" Approach**

The "bucket bailer" approach proceeds from the perspective that client interviewing is like bailing out a boat with a bucket. The client or business wants their boat bailed of the litigation problem, so that the client's boat doesn't sink. It wants the lawyer to either empty or carry the load. It is much more efficient for the client to give first than for the lawyer to give the scope of the problem, and how it is affecting its business, than for the lawyer to guess what is going on. Using the bailing the analogy, it is better for the lawyer to use big buckets to bail out the client's boat, than to use cups or ladles. Question form relates to the size of the bailing instrument. The "bigger" the question, the more efficient the bailing.

The exercise playing "Twenty Questions" helps demonstrate this point. It also reminds the lawyer how important the **form** of the question is to getting the witness to talk (the old who-what-when-where-why approach).

Examples of open ended questions

What can I do for you?	How did it happen?
What happened?	Why did this happen?
What else happened?	When was this?
Describe what happened.	Who was involved?
Explain that to me some more.	Where did the events take place?
Please tell me all you can.	

To guard against making false assumptions, and creating too passive a role for the interviewee (making it too easy for him to fail to disclose threatening information and prolonging the interviewing process), the funnel approach attempts open questions first, and saves more directed questions for follow up, detail, confirmation, and theory verification.

1.2.4 Ice Breaking

If it is true that a willing interviewee provides better, more complete information, faster than a reluctant interviewee, then taking the time to look to the client's comfort is worth some thought and preparation. Remember, the psychiatrist places the interviewee on the couch for good reasons. While the couch is a little much for the lawyer, picking a non-threatening place (around the coffee table on a couch) may facilitate comfort and rapport. Asking after the person's health and welfare, offering a beverage, and talking weather or sports, communicates far more than one might expect. It communicates a broader interest in the client and develops the rapport that can lead to trust and a full and frank conversation.

Also, if you pick the right ice breaker you can get valuable information about the case. (For example, "How's business?" or "You taking a vacation this summer?" can tell you much that may relate to the case.) Ice breaking also sends the message that this person is important to you, rather than some cog in a legal production assembly line.

Leave the **statistical** information to your secretary or receptionist. Develop a routine about **fees**. Usually it is best not to lead with this but to raise it where it may become an issue or at the end when you can make a better assessment of what arrangement you need to make. (You have professional responsibility obligations to explain the nature of your fee structure.)

1.3 The Three-Stage Interview

1. The "Emotional Deck Clearing" stage

2. The "Problem Skeleton (or 'Overview')" stage

3. The "Early Theory Verification (or smaller, 'Ladle')" stage

A three-stage interview is a flexible, useful model for thinking about the interview itself. It balances conflicting goals and incorporates the "bucket bailer" approach.

First is a preliminary problem identification stage, which can be labeled "Emotional Deck Clearing." It is best thought of as a broad survey of the problem and how it is affecting the client and his business. Second is the "Problem Skeleton" or "Overview" stage. The final is "Early Theory Verification," or smaller "Ladle" stage.

1.3.1 The "Emotional Deck Clearing" Stage

The "Emotional Deck Clearing" stage is a time for the witness to tell you what is most important to him for you to hear. It helps the lawyer get an overview of both what the client knows and how he feels about the situation. It also helps the lawyer guard against making false assumptions, and making inappropriate recommendations, comments, asking inartful questions, and becoming prematurely judgmental.

Open ended questions best prompt emotional deck clearing. The idea is to prolong the client's description at least until the client asks for your input. The lawyer should interrupt as little as possible, hold taking notes until the problem overview stage, and use nonverbal probes to try to exhaust the client's knowledge and feelings.

Probes. The following probes, designed to provoke more from the client, are arranged in order of directiveness. The more directive the interviewer's probes, the more the lawyer risks narrowing too quickly and making false assumptions. Training through courses in law school and involvement in other cases are hard to shake (just as other patient cases are hard for doctors to shake when they take patient history), and early narrowing can lead to misdiagnosis.

Silence	
Mm-hmm	
Yes **okay** **I see**	These words can be meant as "I hear you," but may communicate more.
Restatement	Restating actual words of interviewee ("I'm listening to you so carefully I can repeat your exact words").
Clarification	Much more directive because it involves interpretation
	Reflect the feelings and attitudes the client is feeling ("I can understand you must have been angry").
Explanation	Telling the client how things are and how to respond.
Assurance **Reassurance**	Directive because focuses the client's attention ("I hear what you are saying and this is good stuff").

Note taking and/or recording. Taking notes usually does not work well, especially in the first stage of the interview. There is too much going on and the interviewer must establish empathy and listening ability. You can always take notes when you are verifying your theories, or after drafting an interview memo that summarizes facts, by confirming times and dates with the client. Recording an interview is a possible alternative.[3] Check your jurisdiction for whether recordings can be used for impeachment. Assess the taping's effect on the client. (Can you offer taping as a cost savings, so that you need not pull away another lawyer or paralegal to take notes?) A better alternative may be a tablet notebook computer. This kind of laptop sits flat on the desk like a thin book, and the user simply writes in handwriting on the surface. This tablet then folds back so that the computer is configured like a regular notebook with a keyboard and a screen. After the interview is over, the keyboard can be used to label the notes, to add key words for easy searching, and to file the notes with other case records.

1.3.2 The "Problem Skeleton" Stage[4]

During this stage, find a beginning, middle and end to the story. You need a skeleton outline of what happened that you will use to give your story its life and personality, its motivations, and themes. Create a time line and fill in the client's thoughts, feelings, and motivations before, during, and after each key event. Your questions will use time to direct the client to a sequence of events, but then use broad questions as buckets to bail out the client's knowledge of the subject. "How did the situation first come to your attention?" "What steps did you first take to deal with it?" "What did you do immediately after that?" Also be on the look-out for **nonevents** and **lasting conditions**. In addition, think of the problem in terms of its broad topics. "How is this affecting your Management?" "How is it affecting your relations with . . . shareholders, bankers, suppliers, customers?" Bail with open questions first before you go after the details with questions asking for specific information: like time, and who was present, and how long the meetings lasted, and what exactly was said.[5]

---

3. In the event that you use a recorder, a digital recorder is more efficient for this purpose. Digital audio files can be stored, transmitted, and converted to written records more easily than the analog tapes created by older equipment.

4. See §3.2.1 on time lines, infra.

5. See *Lawyers As Counselors: A Client-Centered Approach.* by David A. Binder, Susan C. Price, and Paul Bergman, pps. 171–179 (West Publishing 1991, 2004).

1.3.3 The "Early Theory Verification" Stage

Though you are still very early in the process, you should seek to confirm your understanding of what has been told. Your questioning technique now uses more leading questions. If the answers surprise you, you need to open back up and ask the client to explain, describe, and elaborate on what happened. You should also use restatement of what the client says, and reflection of what the client felt, in order to reach a good understanding, and to guard against your wrong assumptions or conflicting values.

Where appropriate you can start to confirm your **legal theory**, your **factual theory,** and your **theme**. One danger here! Where the client is hungry for assurance, he may hear these confirmations as advice about the success of his case. Also, if no legal research has been done, or the lawyer has no experience with potential statute of limitations, defenses, or opposing conditions and facts, the lawyer should avoid predicting the outcome of the case. Better to involve the client in a process of gathering more facts, explaining that it is premature to predict the outcome, but that the client can be assured of the lawyer's effort on the client's behalf.

Example Closing Statement:

> Why don't you get me copies of the following documents and correspondence? (Make a list.) While you are getting me these materials, I'm going to do some legal research and prepare a fact investigation plan as to where we go from here. I would predict that this work will take approximately ten hours. My billing rate at the firm is $450 per hour, and if I find out it will take longer than ten hours, I will get back to you to see what you want to do. Why don't we then get together in a week and I can look over what you have, and I can counsel you on where we should go from there.

Theory Verification attempts to reach an understanding of the client's position by confirming what has been said. It also is the place where the lawyer can most safely move into the role of writer and producer. More will be said on this in the Witness Interviewing Section.

1.4 Client-Supportive Witness Interviews

There is nothing more important to the lawyer's dual role of fact investigator and advocate than witness interviewing. It is often the beginning lawyer's first face-to-face encounter with the adversarial nature of the practice. Our starting place is a reminder of how uncertain and difficult perception and memory are. It is one of the first lessons taught in many law school classes: How fact witnesses can see things so completely differently from each other, and how even friendly witnesses can come to contradict your client on important issues in the case. The uncertainty and pliability of memory forces the lawyer to again confront his two conflicting roles. Expert handling of the fact witnesses is often crucial to the outcome of the case.

One illustration of the importance of witness interviewing arose in a recent exploding rear-end pickup/gas tank case. The defense trial lawyer and his firm were called into the case late, after much of the discovery had been completed. In brainstorming about the case, the defense trial team came to focus on a factual theory: the plaintiff would have died anyway. In other words, they came to want the jury to believe that the plaintiff was killed from the initial collision with the other car and not from the defendant's design choice in the placement of the gas tank in the rear end of the plaintiff's pickup. The lead defense lawyer became so attached to the theory that he featured it prominently in his opening statement, saying that while he was sorry for the plaintiff's death, the design of the truck had nothing to do with it. The plaintiff was killed instantly on impact.

The first witness called by the plaintiff's counsel was a witness to the accident. After describing the events leading up to impact the plaintiff's lawyer asked, "Then what happened immediately after impact?" Answer. "I saw the truck become engulfed in flames, which spread almost immediately into the driver's compartment. Then I saw the plaintiff struggling to control the vehicle, *and steer it over to the side of the road.*"

Of course, at this point the defendant's factual theory was not worth much, and the defendant's credibility would never recover. The problem is that the defendant had a factual theory that went too far, and that was not verified by one of the key eyewitnesses in the case. The defendant's advocacy story-telling role had become too prominent, to the exclusion of the fact investigator role. The point is subtle. The factual theory that he died from the initial collision, not the fire, was still viable. Where the story went too far was in the lawyer's saying he died instantly.

<•><•><•>

FURTHER READING

Books

Fact Investigation: A Practical Guide to Interviewing, Counseling, and Case Theory Development by Paul J. Zwier and Anthony J. Bocchino (NITA, 2000)

CHAPTER TWO
OTHER FACTS TO SHAPE A LEGAL STRATEGY

I can win an argument on any topic, against any opponent. People know this, and steer clear of me at parties. Often, as a sign of their great respect, they don't even invite me.—Dave Barry, U.S. columnist and humorist (1947–)

Not only must you have done your homework regarding your own client and their facts, you also need to determine how the world-at-large and your opponent perceive the situation. There is no greater inhibitor to dispute resolution than when parties falsely attribute levels of intent and irresponsibility to others.[1] It is vital before turning an accusing finger to first empathize with your opponent in order to frame the right level of response.

2.1 Documents from Opponents and Third Parties

It is necessary to think strategically about collecting documents from your opponents. If you have already engaged in a document management process of your own, one solution is to negotiate a process where by an equivalent document exchange will be done by the other parties. It is important to understand that there are various document search processes that may affect the quality of the document searches. These can be affected by the way the documents are scanned and the language searches that have been used to sort and flag the key documents. If each side can engage in a shared process for document exchange, each may reach a similar level of trust concerning the documents produced by the documents. This is the process contemplated by the Federal Rules of Civil Procedure and its mandatory disclosure provisions of all documents that relate to claims pled and any defenses. The FRCP rule 26(f) Conference is designed to facilitate this exchange and provide a forum for mediating any difficulties that may arise

Of course, one way to test the legitimacy of what has been exchanged is to do your own search of the other side's documents.

---

1. *See* chapter 5, *infra.*

First you need to determine the scope of your search. How many years do you need to go back and how many divisions of a particular company may be involved. Again, once you have the world of documents, you need to convert them into a searchable data base. In a sense, you drill into these documents for a core sample, like you drill for a core sample to find valuable minerals. Your OCR support can help you frame your language search techniques and your samples to most efficiently produce the key documents.

In the appropriate case, you may also want to search the Internet for other publicly produced documents and check these against what you are receiving from the opposition. Publicly traded companies make press releases, SEC and national exchange disclosures, and hold shareholder meetings. In addition, look for magazine interviews, newspaper reports, and television interviews that may have been conducted with key employees. You may also want to search the internet for Web sites for company information, bloggers, chat rooms, etc. for employee statements that relate to your dispute.

2.2 Corroborating Witnesses

As soon as you can, you need to determine the level of trust you can place in your opponent's documents by interviewing other witnesses who will be able to corroborate what you are finding. To start with, it is essential that the lawyer understand how their role will change depending upon the nature of the witness being interviewed.

2.2.1 Contrast with Friendly Witnesses

When dealing with a friendly witness, the lawyer's first goal is to obtain information. The lawyer needs to obtain and preserve all favorable facts. He needs to obtain and subordinate (not suppress) unfavorable information. He needs to obtain leads to other facts, evidence and witnesses. He also needs to preserve information by ensuring that he has the ability to locate it again. In addition, the lawyer needs to establish rapport. This rapport not only helps him get information, but it can enlist partisan support which can engender a number of side benefits, including moral support for the client, as well as a certain unapologetic enthusiasm for the lawyer and the case.

2.2.2 **Unfriendly Witnesses**

If the witness is unfriendly, or at best neutral, the lawyer has many of the same goals as when the witness is friendly. At the same time though, the lawyer wants to obtain information about the sources or bases of any adverse bias the witness might have. The lawyer also needs to be on the lookout to preserve impeaching utterances. Rapport still may help get information and entice the witness into disclosing his bias and his impeaching utterances, but if these techniques fail, then the lawyer must ask more pointed questions. Finally, with the unfriendly witness, the lawyer needs to evaluate the critical information that the witness possesses to determine whether the witness threatens either the legal theory, the factual theory, or the theme of the case.

2.2.3 **Contrasting Questioning Strategies**

For example, if dealing with a friendly witness—an insurance broker, on behalf of an insurance company—the earlier-described interview model (ice breaker, emotional deck clearing, problem skeleton outline, early theory verification, and partnered closing) should work very well. The lawyer should be able to say things like:

> You've worked with this insurance company for a number of years?

> What has been your relationship with them?

> How's business?

> You mentioned termite protection. In your experience, how often has an excess policy ever covered termites?

> Please tell me about what types of coverage is provided in an excess policy like the one you sold in this case.

> Tell me about your meeting with the risk management team at the company.

> Describe the steps you took after your interview
> with company officials, in preparing the contract
> for signature.

If rapport has developed and the broker believes the lawyer is on his side, the broker should be forthcoming with complete and comprehensive answers to these questions.

In contrast, hostile or borderline witnesses are unlikely to respond very well to open ended questions or to the "bucket bailer" approach to interviewing. They may prefer not to answer, or to wait the lawyer out by answering simply and in a misleading manner. Their narrative statements are more likely to be vague and conclusory. For example, if the broker were asked the above questions by the insured's lawyer, the broker would likely answer, "I just love my relationship with the insurance company. I have always found them to pay quickly on legitimate claims." If the broker is in a continuing relationship with the insurance company, he is likely to be hesitant to say more than how good business was and how honest the insurance company representative was, for fear that his answers would get back to the insurance company.

In addition, the broker's early answers to these open ended and general questions could cause him to infer other answers consistent with these earlier answers, compounding the bias effects in the witness's statements. For example, once he has committed himself that things are great with the insurance company, and that the insurance company is an honest shop, it would be much harder for him to later admit that he remembered the insurance company representative promising that coverage would include the events at issue in the case.

Invert the order in which you use bailing instruments to bail out the witness's information. You need to get in the boat before you can bail. Start with narrower questions and get answers that can be quickly and easily given. Also, by using more leading type questions, it is more likely to avoid the false inferences that can arise from inferential and biased reconstruction of events. Using "cans" and "ladles" starts the question more at the theory verification part of the questioning. For example, the insured's lawyer, after some ice breaking, might ask the broker more leading questions, earlier.

These questions might include:

> You got a commission on a sale to this insured?

> As a broker, you wanted to make sure there was a fit between what the insurance company was selling and what the insured needed?

> You were familiar with the business the insured was in?

> Did their risk management director strike you as competent in his field?

> Would it have been unusual for a risk manager looking to protect his company's business to want to customize insurance to his company's particular risks?

While the leading question is dangerous, its adversarial nature can be cut by editing out the traditional lawyer-like signals of hostility. The fact investigator should not be asking, "It's true that . . ." "It's correct that . . ." or finish off the statements with, " . . . isn't that correct?"

2.3 Inhibitors and Techniques in Response

If you are able to get to the borderline or neutral witness early enough, before they have been biased against you, be very careful in your planning and approach in order not to scare away the witness. Essential to this planning is to again review the reasons why a witness might not want to talk to you at all. Binder and Price catalogue the reasons why a witness might not want to talk to you as inhibitors, and it is important to diagnose the likely inhibitors so you can prepare a response, should they arise. We will spend some time going over what they are, so that you can prepare appropriate strategies to overcome them, should you see them.

2.3.1 Personal Threat

The witness may be inhibited to reveal information that threatens self-esteem. For example, an insurance broker might not want to reveal specific information in his employment history where he failed to live up to either his own or the insurance carrier's expectations. Other examples could include the fact that the broker may not have ever read the contract between the client

Also, where an insurance broker is answering questions from a lawyer opposed to the broker's client, the broker will not likely want to be critical of the broker's client. On the other hand, to admit that he did not read a policy he sold would make him look only concerned about the sale and his commission, and not concerned with whether he was providing insurance that fit a customer's needs.

If the lawyer diagnoses that the witness is afraid of personal embarrassment, then the lawyer should offer reassurance about their role as advocate, not judge. If confidentiality can be offered, this can often alleviate the hesitation. Where it can't be offered (see discussion below), the lawyer has to use his skills to develop rapport. These skills include the use of nonverbal probes, and active listening techniques to get the witness to feel complemented and safe, and reveal what is really of concern.

2.3.2 Select A Neutral Location

A quick review of these probes is in order here. The first is to choose a place for the interview that is non-threatening. Don't call the witness into your office, but go out where they are comfortable, where they feel safe. Pick a time when they are likely to be relaxed, like early evening after they have eaten. Many nonprofessional witnesses don't like to be bothered at work or right before dinner when they are rushing around doing family chores. On the other hand, meeting someone for drink after work, at their favorite watering hole, can provide a desirable atmosphere.

2.3.3 Prepare An Ice Breaker

The second key is to again prepare an ice breaker. Pick a common friend or shared interest to discuss. Give each of you a chance to relax and get to know the other's habits of speech and manners of behavior.

2.3.4 **Understanding**

Third, establish that your goal is to reach an understanding of the witness's knowledge and feeling for the subject. More will be said about this in the section on listening. Use silence, eye contact, head nods, "mm-hmms," restatement, and reflection. Wait the witness out. He has the same needs for catharsis and meaning that we talked about with regard to client interviewing. Premature questioning or judgmental responses can kill a good narrative. Use head nods and silence to wait out the witness, giving them time to choose their own words, and order their thoughts. Don't let him off the hook, or come to his rescue just when he is about to speak. Restate what you hear, and if this does not work, reflect the feelings you see on the witness's face, to show that you care to reach a complete understanding and that his feelings, as well as his thoughts, are vital to this process. These probes often take time to work, and the best thing is to lend a sympathetic ear and exercise patience. Manage your own feelings of discomfort or impatience by expressing the willingness to wait the witness out, and force him to take all the time he needs to tell you about his particular circumstances.

2.3.5 **Perceived Job Threat**

The witness will sometimes fear that certain information could threaten his or her continued employment, (or own responsibility) and makes him hesitant to answer the lawyer's questions. For example, if the environmental compliance officer in a company admits he knows of noncompliance, he could lose his job. If you work for the company, and anticipate such a situation where an employee is concerned he may lose his job over what he did, there are a number of ways you might respond. First, if there is some already existing evidence that he did make a mistake, you might first go to the organization's in-house counsel and ask them how they want to treat the employee. Perhaps they will waive their conflict and offer assurances to the employee that they "are all in this together." It may then be possible for the lawyer to offer joint representation and promise confidentiality and immunity from firing in exchange for the witnesses's cooperation and truthful testimony.

The organization might express an unwillingness to make such promises until it learns more detailed information about what the witness actually did. If this is the case, the lawyer needs to guard against creating the reasonable impression in the witness that the witness's statements are confidential before they are actually confidential.

Along the same line, the lawyer needs to be careful to state who he represents and what is and what is not confidential from the employer. In appropriate cases the lawyer might suggest counsel to the employee—if fairness dictates—that the employee is under suspicion. In any event, the lawyer should seek advice from the client on how to handle the potential conflict of interest before interviewing employees who are fact witnesses.

Again, in the situation involving the hypothetical insurance broker, if you are representing the insurance carrier, the broker might be afraid to admit that he made a mistake. As lawyer, if you were aware of this you could prepare to follow-up and ask specific questions about exactly what the broker said, did, and wrote, and to whom. Otherwise, the investigator has a tendency to become satisfied with conclusory statements of good positions because they fit the lawyer's theory of the case. If there is some lurking conversation or evidence of the witness's true memory, the lawyer needs to know that up front.

2.4 **Barriers**

In this case, you are arguably dealing with the client's agent. Again, conflict of interest raises its head. While joint representation is often pursued in these cases, it is important to ask up front whether it makes sense for the broker and the carrier to be represented by the same law firm.

While separate representation raises the possibility of finger pointing, joint defenses also raise some difficult conflicts between individual partners and the organization as a whole. The choice is often left to the client, but the professional responsibility codes also suggest that the lawyer first "reasonably conclude" that the parties are not in an actual conflict. If the lawyer can not reasonably conclude that the broker and the carrier are not in actual conflict, then joint representation should not even be attempted.

Even if the parties are in a potential conflict that has been disclosed and waived, there still might be instances when the potential conflict becomes actual, and the lawyer is forced to withdraw. If the lawyer at all suspects that she will inevitably be forced to withdraw from the case, joint representation should not be considered even from the start.

So joint representation is possible, assuming the lawyer has disclosed the conflict to the broker and the insurer and as long as the lawyer remains aware of the possibility that withdrawal may be required down the line. The lawyer should also realize his interest or bias may cause him to not pursue evidence that puts him into an actual conflict. The lawyer's bias can create an impediment to uncovering damaging testimony.

2.4.1 Role Expectations

The witness may be inhibited by his understanding of what behavior is appropriate within certain relationships. Just as you act certain ways toward your parents, in-laws, teachers, or new acquaintances, the witness might feel and say different things to you because of who you are, and vice-versa. If an associate goes in to speak to a senior vice president of a major company when doing due diligence, it will be hard to ask tough, pertinent questions that question the VP's decision making.

While rapport building might be necessary for frank disclosure, the associate might feel that the VP thinks the associate is wasting his time with chit-chat. An especially cost-conscious client may feel this way. The associate may feel forced to sacrifice frankness and rapport, for time savings. Unfortunately, this can compound the costs in defending the lawsuit by having to return to the VP to clear up the lawyer's understanding of the case.

Better to make your reasoning explicit as to why you are requiring a block of the VP's time. Tell the VP that if you are to play on the same team, you must understand how he thinks (thought), and feels (felt), about the events relevant to the case. Tell him you have been diligent in seeking out the information from other sources, but that only he can answer for his thoughts and actions during the relevant time period, and it is his job to do so.

Depending on the witness's role, the lawyer may be cast in different roles. The lawyer may have to take the listening role in some situations, and the more talkative, apparently controlling, and dominant role with other witnesses. With the stereotypical hesitant witness who is intimidated by your lawyer status, you must work on persuading the witness about his importance to your task.

Two persuasion statements that often help follow.

Describe who you work for, and blame them for having to bother the witness. For example, you might say:

> My supervisor sent me to talk to you. He says you know all about how these things work and what happened. I can't go back to her empty handed or I'm in real trouble. Can you help me out?

Sharing the perspective of an employee that has an employer telling them what to do can build a good bond with the blue-collar witness. And the best part of it is that it is true. It is your job to find out what happened, and you are likely to be evaluated on how well you do it.

Use a variation of the above with a subtle threat. The technique is called "raising the witness's expectations." Remind the witness of his or her position to know the facts. The fact investigator might say to the broker,

> Our records show that you were at the meeting and that your job was to help the carrier reach an understanding as to what it was insuring. What did you do to fulfill your responsibilities toward the carrier in that meeting?

In other words, remind the witness that you know they were there as part of their job responsibilities. Your implicit persuasive statement is that you will not accept that they don't know or don't remember, because it would not be consistent with the expectations of their employer, you, or themselves in similar circumstances.

2.4.2 **Etiquette Barrier**

The witness may think that there are certain things that one just does not tell certain other people; that it is not polite to say those things in public. Closely related to etiquette are the witnesses' motivations to protect the privacy of another person. Witnesses may feel that loyalty demands that they not speak ill of another. For example, this can cause all kinds of problems in an employment sexual harassment case. Employees may not feel that they can talk about other people's sexual relationships. Managers may be protecting other people's privacy, including the spouses of those involved. Etiquette may make it very difficult to find out who was sleeping with whom, for how long, and with what motivation.

There is again a short story here that may help make the point. Lawyers for the defendants in the *Dalkon Shield* cases were often baffled by how the company's product made it to the market, if it promoted infection like the plaintiffs claimed it did. In investigating the steps defendants' investigators took in testing the product, they ran into the following repeated behavior: Someone would ask about the testing done on the Dalkon Shield. Someone would make a joke about doing some "additional testing" on the women at the plant. The embarrassment caused by the joke, combined with the etiquette threat of discussing the testing of a sex-related birth control product, seemed to cause investigators to fail to follow up on their due diligence regarding the testing of the product.

Whether in domestic or commercial disputes, the motivations of the parties and their behavior often raise subjects in conversations that require the lawyer to look impolite, or impolitic, to pursue them. Yet it is the job of the fact investigator to learn how to professionally pursue the answers to these impolite questions. The fact investigator must learn how to stay serious and focused on the subject matter at hand.

"How many employees did you sleep with, Ms. Manager?" "What were their names?" "When did you sleep with them?" "How long after having sexual intercourse with Mr. X did he stop working for you?" Tone, demeanor, and seriousness of purpose all contribute to success in fact investigation. And it is necessary that they be virtues and behavior you choose to evidence, long before you are responsible for actually asking the questions. In addition, the lawyer should state that he doesn't mean to pry, and empathize with the intrusive nature of the questions, but the need to prepare and defend make it the lawyer's job to pursue these lines of inquiry.

2.4.3 **Trauma**

The witness's answer to your questions may evoke unpleasant memories. They may experience a certain amount of trauma in remembering what happened. If the witness saw the accident, knew the deceased, or helped get a person fired, it may be hard to get a clear understanding of what the witness knows because of all he was (and is) feeling.

One of the major techniques for dealing with trauma is counter intuitive. Many of us feel very uncomfortable and out of control when we see someone else lose control of his emotions. But in the context of an interview, instead of running from or suppressing these strong emotions, it is sometimes much better to get the witness to express them. Again, what is at work here is catharsis. If the witness feels free to express the emotion, he is often thereafter more willing to work at remembering all the facts and circumstances that led to his feelings. If the depth of the witness's feeling is not understood, he may have more of a selective memory of the events as he intends to persuade the lawyer about the legitimacy of his feelings. By reflecting the feelings the lawyer sees and hears in the voice and face of the witness, the witness can be prompted to express those feelings and clarify them. (More will be said about this technique, in response to the "greater need" inhibitor, described below.)

2.4.4 **Perceived Irrelevance**

Sometimes the witness does not have the energy to summon up the detailed answer you are looking for because the witness simply does not see how the detail is relevant. The witness may think that there is nothing wrong with dumping used oil down the drain; that it's done all the time. Why should she mention it during an environmental audit? The witness is not trying to be evasive, lie, or hide something from the lawyer. She just doesn't know how it is relevant.

Remember that lawyers have an expanded sense of relevance (and plaintiff's lawyers, in particular, of behavior indicators and of causation) that the witness may not share. By using time lines and expectation, the lawyer can start to overcome a witness's feelings of perceived irrelevance. If the lawyer takes the time to tell the witness of his or her need for all the data, the importance that the witness be clear and precise (because the lawyer need deal in a world of proof, where he or she isn't the focus of persuasion, but rather another audience), often he can motivate the witness inhibited by the witness's perceptions of what is relevant.

2.4.5 **Greater Need**

The witness may have a greater need to talk about some other subject than the one on the questioning lawyer's mind at the time. This greater need can also affect the listening skills and the energy level the witness is using to summon up answers to the lawyer's questions. For example, an insurance broker who has been offered a job by the carrier is likely to be much more interested in what the lawyer knows about his impending job offer, than in whether he remembers reading the contract between the carrier and the insured. Or in a child custody case, the mother could be more concerned about preventing spousal abuse than focusing on the evidence she has that she is the better parent. The greater the immediate need, the more difficulty the witness will have in attending to the lawyer's questions.

Again, lawyers need to be able to draw out these greater needs for the sake of both understanding the witness's perspectives, and to help the witness become more exact, precise, and objective about what she knows. Active listening, empathy, (not fake sympathy, but a genuine understanding of the witness position) and reflection of feelings should provide the "emotional deck clearing" that the witness needs, in order to focus more completely on providing the lawyer with information about what happened.

2.4.6 **Time and Money**

The witness could have concerns about his time and the cost of getting involved. He might feel he is unable to afford the time off work if he is to become involved as a witness. He may have childcare concerns or other family priorities that interfere with giving the lawyer the time it takes to remember with precision, what he knows. These are legitimate and important concerns that may have to be addressed with sensitivity and planning, in order to overcome the resistance that these inhibitions engender.

2.4.7 Forgetting

It may seem obvious, but memories fade and witnesses forget. To the lawyer who has lived with a case day-in and day-out for months, at times this fact is hard to remember. Many lawyers may take the witness's hesitation as evasiveness or cooperation with the other side. It is often neither, but is just a simple failing of memory, and a witness's concern that she will make a mistake. In fact, in reviewing of hundreds of lawyers' and law students' interviews, this seems to be a prevalent mistake. Often the lawyer misreads the witness's hesitation as evasiveness and goes on the attack. The lawyer then threatens or cajoles, and ends up making the witness even more confused and uncertain, and additionally defensive and in no mood to cooperate.

2.5 Questioning and Memory Retrieval

Remember that memory involves at least three things:

1. **Original information**—that which was perceived and understood at the time that the event happened.

2. **External information**—that which the observer later learned or was told but didn't observe themselves.

3. **Inferences** that a person makes from what he observed which they then come to know as part of their memory of the event.

As psychologist Elizabeth Loftus explains in her research on human memory, external factors can create distortions that affect a person's memory of an event.[2] She shows how cross-racial identification can be affected, how photos can be biased, how weapon focus can mislead, how the witness often unconsciously transfers other information directed at another person altogether onto the

---

2. Elizabeth F. Loftus, *Surprising New Insights Into How We Remember and Why We Forget* (Addison-Wesley Pub. Co., 1980); Elizabeth F. Loftus, *Eye Witness Testimony*, (Harvard University Press 1996.)

person they say they saw. She also shows how the witness's previous expectations about what would happen can interfere with memory. Finally, while a certain amount of strong motivation or emotional arousal can heighten accuracy, at some point stress or fear interferes with ability of the witness to accurately observe an event in the first place.

More importantly for our purposes, Loftus also show how questions (and therefore questioners) themselves can affect memory. For example:

> **The way a question is phrased can affect estimates people will give.** The question "Do you get headaches frequently, and if so, how often?" produces an average response of 2.2 times per week.
>
> The question "Do you get headaches occasionally, and if so, how often?" changes the average response to 0.7 times week.
>
> "Did you see a broken headlight?" versus "Did you see *the* broken headlight?" produces a response to the second question that is more likely to say he saw a broken headlight, even when there was none.
>
> **The way an earlier question is asked can influence the way later questions are answered.** For example, Loftus showed her subjects a movie of an auto accident. After the movie she asked the subjects questions. Some were asked about the collision using the verb "smashed." Some were asked using only the verb "hit." One week later, when these same people were asked "Did you see the broken glass?," sixteen out of fifty of the "smashed" subjects said they saw broken glass. Only seven of fifty of the "hit" people said they saw broken glass. There was no broken glass.
>
> **Loftus showed that 17.3 percent of subjects will say they saw a barn, where there was no barn, if earlier asked,** "How fast was the car going on the country road when it passed the barn?" Only 2.7

percent will see the barn when asked only "How fast was the car going on the country road?"

Look what happens when you change the verb in the question *"How fast was the car going when it (verb) into the other car?"* The question was designed to illicit a witness's estimate of speed. The following chart shows how varying the verb can effect estimates of speed.

Verb	Mean estimate of miles per hour
Contacted	31.8
Hit	34.0
Bumped	38.1
Collided	39.3
Smashed	40.8

Look at what happens when people are asked about seeing stop signs. In a video showing "A" involved in an auto accident, where "A" had a stop sign, subjects were asked the following two questions: "How fast was "A" going when he turned right?," and "How fast was "A" going when he ran the stop sign?" Later in the questionnaire, when asked whether they saw a stop sign, 35 percent of the first group said they saw a stop sign, and 53 percent of the second group said they did. The second group's ability to recall seemed to be improved by the earlier question.

Questioners seem to be able to create things in some people's minds. Subjects were shown a film of eight people in a classroom. After the film, half were asked, "Was the leader of the twelve people male or female?" Half were asked, "Was the leader of the four people male or female?" One week later, the first group was asked how many people were in the class—they said nine. The second group was asked the same question—they said six. They seemed to be averaging in response to the earlier question.

When asked "Did the demonstrators say anything?," versus "Did the militants say anything?" one week later, the groups were more likely to remember violence of some sort.

People were even seen to change the colors they see. They will change blue to bluish green. If the car was blue, and if they were earlier asked a question that assumes the car's color was green, they will answer "bluish green."

Once people change their impressions, it becomes harder and harder for them to change back. Advertisers know it. Aetna and St. Paul insurance ads prove it. If juries have seen Aetna and St. Paul ads, even briefly, their awards are likely to be lowered. They import what they see into their understanding and it interferes with their judgment, and their view of the facts. Of course this is nothing new, but Loftus places squarely before lawyers the ethical problems of manipulating witnesses into telling different stories about past events.

Loftus teaches us to look for ways the memory can be shaped. In his role as a fact-finder, the lawyer must be careful his witness's memory hasn't made them blind to the hard facts that may come back and contradict them later.

2.5.1 Fixes for Memory Inhibitors

One fix that Loftus herself suggests is to use **memory flood**. If the aim is to get the witness to accurately remember what occurred in the past, then he needs to be oriented to time and place before he reconstructs his memory about what happened. Your use of a time line or documents can greatly facilitate this process. Show him the time line, and orient him to time and place by giving him time to recall where he was, who he was with, and what else was going on, in order for him to carefully reconstruct what happened. Interestingly enough, the open ended question that calls for a narrative can be unproductive and in fact can lead to inferential confusion. The witness might too easily infer what he knew, and when he knew it, in reference to how he feels about it now, or what he says in a conclusory response to the open ended question. Therefore, if you suspect a witness will have difficulty because of the passage of time or the existence of external information that could lead to confusion, it is better to first ask more pointed questions that allow the witness to orient himself regarding time and place. The chance that he will be accurate improves greatly.

2.5.2 **Unwanted Recollection**

If, however, the lawyer does not want any recollection, he might reverse the inferences in his questions by first evoking the circumstances that might make it difficult for the witness to remember. For example, if it was dark, and things happened fast, or if it was along time ago, and a lot has happened since them, reminding the witness of these fact will suggest that the witness might not recall what happened and lead to a response that he doesn't. From that, the witness might build an inference chain that he doesn't know other more specific answers to what people said or heard or did.

Again, there is no magic here, and there is danger in trying to make a bad fact go away, when there are chances that it exists. Still, there are circumstances where the advocate in the lawyer with the borderline or hostile witness has an obligation to zealously represent the client. Where a witness remembers facts that run against the client's memory, or seem to contradict other statements he has made, as a questioner, the lawyer must look hard for independent verification of the memory: other witnesses, whether the memory was recorded (and if so, where and when), and any other facts or circumstances that support the opposing witness' view. (After all, we don't want a witness to later say he saw the plaintiff drive the car to the side of the road, if our theory is that he died on impact.) But if there is no independent verification, and if the witness's memory could have been affected by external information, it is the role of the advocate to discover that external information and to impeach the witness's story. What the lawyer needs to be able to do is to move between roles; to be a rapport building, listening fact investigator, and a questioning, challenging, and creative advocate.

2.6 **Planning To Use Other Facilitators**

As stated above, picking the right time and place can go along way to alleviating witnesses' legitimate concerns about their personal use of time. Yet these might be excuses to some other inhibition that keeps the witness from talking. Perhaps hesitation is only an honest difficulty in memory retrieval. Perhaps it is a conscious bias that causes the memory to be faulty.

One way of diagnosing the inhibition is to use facilitators with gradually escalating consequences to help the lawyer determine the true nature of the inhibition. For example, the lawyer could first engage in what psychologists call an "altruistic appeal." The lawyer could plan to deliver a short one-paragraph statement of the strengths of their case, and then make an altruistic deal. For example, if a lawyer represents a client, Homestead Properties, Inc., which bought an insurance policy from Manhattan Fire & Casualty Company to cover problems that might arise from their manufactured home business, and Homestead cannot get Manhattan to pay on the policy, the fact investigating lawyer might start out this way:

> I represent Homestead, who is facing bankruptcy because it can't get payment from Manhattan on the excess policy it paid on for over six years. Homestead needed excess coverage for manufacturing defects because in was mass manufacturing homes, much like a car maker mass manufacturers cars. It followed Florida guidelines regarding application of pesticide for termites, only to find that Florida's guidelines were inadequate for its type of construction. Unbeknownst to Homestead, termites had infested and destroyed over $30 million worth of its homes. We appreciate your willingness to talk to us in this case. There are powerful forces at work against Homestead, and it is not everyone who would be willing to stand up and say what they know. Thank you for agreeing to talk.

The power of the persuasive statement on the borderline witness cannot be overestimated. It tells the witness not just what side you are on, but that you are on the side of truth and justice. If you have a witness who really does not know what he knows, or hasn't yet developed a point of view, such a well-told statement could create a general premise from which he is willing to infer all sorts of things.

If this fails, the lawyer can make time savings statements. A fact investigator for Homestead could say, "We are still early on in the process and we are trying to decide what position we will take in this case. If you talk to us now, there may be no need to talk later. If we can show Homestead what role you played, and what role Manhattan played in creating the contract, then Homestead can decide what it should do." Implicitly, the lawyer is saying, "If we can just have a few minutes of your time now, this may all go away."

Or, the lawyer may raise the stakes:

> Look, you either talk to me now, or I'll have to subpoena you. Then other lawyers will be present, and you'll be placed under oath, and then you'll have to answer my questions. I don't want that and you don't want that. I don't think this will take too long. Please answer my questions.

Of course threats may backfire. They certainly will dampen your efforts at establishing rapport. But if you are serious in your need for the information, you might also investigate even more immediate threats. If you are investigating on behalf of Manhattan, for example, you may especially need the insurance broker's cooperation, because some other witness is unavailable. If the particular witness has a job (or insurance policy) that requires him to cooperate, this fact can be used as a threat to force the issue. Even here, use the threat in stages.

> Look, I don't want to be in a position of reporting back to the boss (or insurance company) that you are not cooperating with my investigation. What do you say we take the time now and sort out what happened?

If these efforts fail, shift over into damage control. You should explore whether the witness has already given a statement to the other side. You should find out whether the witness has been told not to talk to you. You should also be careful to record any other impeaching and biasing statements that the witness might make in refusing to talk to you. Does he protest because "he might lose his job," "the target is his friend," "he doesn't know anything," or "he is scared?" Any of these statements are useful for impeachment, if they are preserved in a form that makes them usable at trial. Confirm what you have heard. Write it down. Reread it to the witness and ask him whether you have accurately heard the reason he is giving for not talking to you.

This raises some additional planning issues before the fact investigator goes to meet the witness. Often the investigator goes armed with an official looking legal pad and pen, and madly records down verbatim what the witness tells him. But using these techniques prematurely increases the likelihood that the investigator won't establish any kind of rapport, or that he will forget to look interested, or nonjudgmental, or maintain eye contact, or head nod, or appropriately respond to what he sees in the witness's face while the witness is talking.

Researchers tell us that communication is a physical act, and that only a small part of it is what we actually say. Our feelings will often be evident in the way we say something and convey additional weight and meaning.[3] Often the nuance, subtlety, or conflicting feeling comes from the hand gestures, eyes, or expression on the face. These all go unobserved if the investigator's head is buried in his yellow pad. Better for the interviewer to develop habits that allow him "to listen with his eyes," rather than just his ears.

Other techniques that allow you to give full attention to the interviewee and which have some prove success are:

1. Wait until after you are done, then offer to write up what has been said, "to make sure I've got it right."

   The witness can look it over and make any corrections, and then sign the statement. This way, the witness can feel safe and listened-to while talking, and further feel that words weren't put in his mouth in that he will have a final say in what he signs.

2. Another technique is to bring along a third person to take notes.

---

3. Douglas Stone, Bruce Patton, Sheila Heen, *Difficult Conversations: How To Discuss what Matters Most* (Viking Press, 1999).

3. A third option is to tape the conversation.

The dangers with these last techniques should not be overlooked. Not only can they impede the witness in his telling, the technique could be illegal if done without permission. In New York for example, you must tell a person you are recording the conversation, or you can't use it against him, and you can be sued for invasion of his privacy. Also, because the lawyer does not know yet what the witness will say, the lawyer could be preserving damaging testimony against his client. It is most often better to interview first and then record in the form of statement or later deposition, if the need arises. Otherwise it is better to first try face-to-face rapport building techniques, than to go in using your adversarial manner. You can always become more adversarial. If you start adversarial, it is unlikely that becoming friendly later will work.

❬•❭❬•❭❬•❭

FURTHER READING

Books

Deborah Stone, Bruce Patton, and Sheila Heen, *Difficult Conversations: How to Discuss What Matters Most* (Vantage, 1999).

David A. Binder, Paul Bergman and Susan C. Price, *Lawyer as Counselor: A Client-Centered Approach* (1990).

David A. Binder and Paul Bergman, *Fact Investigation* (1984).

CHAPTER THREE
CASE ANALYSIS FOR REFINING A STRATEGY

To win by strategy is no less the role of a general than to win by arms.
—Julius Caesar (100–44 B.C.)

Throughout litigation and deal making, the lawyer and the client are gaining information that allows them to understand their situation and define the problem. Key to effective strategic decision making is to solve the right problem, and you can't solve the right problem if you don't understand it. Key, however, to this understanding in the context of the lawyer's world, is an understanding of the end game; for the deal maker, it is what happens if the deal falls apart; for the litigator, it is the trial. Each end-game analysis is essential to what defines the legal nature of the client's problem. When the client asks, "Should I settle this case," or "Should I enter this deal," he is asking in part, "What are the chances of winning at trial, or what are my chances that if something goes wrong I am protected?" At the same time, the lawyer is looking for facts to help the client evaluate the nature of their problem and define the problem or deal, in relationship to the end game.

3.1 A Litigator's Paradoxical Roles

To see how these roles play out, let's examine the litigator roles, in particular. There are two somewhat paradoxical models the litigator has when conducting fact investigation and doing case analysis. The first of these roles is that of a researcher who is trying to discover what happened in the past. The investigator tries to discover what happened—what people's behavior and actions were, what they said and didn't say, what they knew and didn't know, what they intended and didn't intend, what they remembered or perceived, what they didn't perceive, and what they recorded or did not record.

At the same time lawyers are the creators and producers of a persuasive story. They are often less concerned with what actually happened than with which story they can tell to allow the client to maximize his freedom. Lawyers play the role of blocker and protector, as well as interpreter and spokesperson on behalf of the client. They are the public relations agent or "ad man" for the client within the context of the legal system. They are at all times the negotiator, advocate, and persuader on behalf of the client.

How does the lawyer reconcile himself to these two often paradoxical roles, in the context of fact investigation planning and analyzing cases? To answer this question the lawyer needs to look ahead to the end of the process. While it is true that most cases settle (latest estimates are 99 percent for civil cases filed in federal court), all litigators are intimately aware that the client's case could end up in court. They build their case with that in mind. Even where their cases settle, the lawyers frame to their opponent what they say happened in much the same way that they would tell the court in opening statement and closing argument about why they should win. So what is it that the end game requires of the lawyer? The lawyer must prepare to present the client's case with three different theories in mind:

the **legal theory**,

factual theory, and

persuasive theory or **theme**

Understanding the role and interplay of these three theories in the end game of litigation will instruct the lawyer on how they are to carry out their role as fact investigator, analyze the case, and best prepare the case for settlement or for final trial. (This is also instructive for the deal maker. The deal maker needs to both investigate the client's business and that of the other party to the deal. The lawyer also needs to understand both the legal rules involved in the deal and the deal's "pitch" or place in the marketplace of deals.)

3.1.1 Legal Theory

It may seem obvious and even trivial to say that a lawyer needs to have a legal theory in mind when he conducts fact investigation, but many judges and juries recall trials presented when the lawyer didn't seem to be clear about which legal theory he was presenting. It is very important to understand how a clear legal theory can help persuade a decision maker to decide the case in favor of the lawyer's client. The secret to a good legal theory is that it carries with it the power of logic—the power of the syllogism.

3.1.1.1 Syllogisms and Legal Interpretation

Syllogisms, you may remember, comes from analytic philosophy. A common example of a syllogism that is much discussed in beginning undergraduate philosophy classes is:

Major premise: All men are mortal

Minor premise: Socrates is a man

Conclusion: Socrates is mortal

The above conclusion is said to be logically entailed, or necessary. The minor premise is included in the major premise and the conclusion is driven or required by the major premise.

The advocate tries to create this same sense of logic, the logic of entitlement, by stating a major premise incorporating the facts as they think them to be. For example:

Major premise: The law is that where a competitor disparages (with malice makes untruthful statements about) another's product and causes the manufacturer loss of sales, then the disparager is liable.

Minor premise: In this case, Best Homes maliciously disparaged Homestead's products, causing Homestead to lose sales to buyers who otherwise would have bought Homestead's product.

Conclusion: Best Homes is liable for their actions in this case.

Of course, as every lawyer knows, and as Aristotle pointed out thousands of years earlier, there are very few situations in the real world where a conclusion is logically entailed. Either there is some ambiguity in the law, (in a defamation case, did your opposition have malice, knowledge, and or substantial doubts of the falsity of what it said?) or there is some major problem factually, (whether your competitor disparaged your product, or caused the loss in sales.) This second point regarding factual difficulties gets us ahead of our present topic. The issue here is that legal problems are almost always subject to problems of legal interpretation that make the law indeterminate or at least create uncertainty and that the attempted legal syllogism more often than not fails as a matter of strict logic.

3.1.1.2 **Paramount Communications, Inc. v. QVC**[1]

Still, the importance of a syllogistic reasoning, or having a legal theory, should not be underestimated. Take for example the case of *Paramount Communications, Inc. v. QVC*. In that case the lead litigator for one of the parties decided to try to predict what law the Delaware Supreme Court would adopt in order to determine whether the corporate board had adequately protected shareholder rights. The board had been accused by the shareholders of breaching a duty of care to them by approving a merger between the defendant company and a takeover company without providing adequate assurance they were getting the shareholders top dollar for their shares. The lead litigator predicted that the Delaware Supreme Court would eventually adopt a standard that would require the board of directors to "shop" the company, or put the company "in play" or "up for bid," in order to fulfill their fiduciary duties to the shareholders. During depositions of the defendant company's board of directors, the litigation team continually asked the board members whether they thought it was their duty to shop the company before accepting the offeror's bid for the target company. The board members said no. When the Delaware Supreme Court agreed with the litigator's prediction—that it was the board's duty to shop the company—the result was logically entailed. Having predicted correctly what the law would be, the lawyers knew the questions to ask to create the appropriate syllogism. The board members gave their answers unaware of the consequences of their answers. Having a clear legal theory can therefore drive the result by making the case "easy" for the decision maker.

---

1. 637 A. 2d. 34 (1983).

3.1.1.3 **Developing A Legal Theory**

For the beginning litigator, the feeling that he ought to have a legal theory before he does discovery can create other feelings of inadequacy and uncertainty that can lead to paralysis in the fact investigation process. But there are a number of practical steps that lawyers can take to at least start to identify their possible legal theories and allow them to start anticipating the areas of fact investigation. For example, the plaintiff's counsel or solo practitioner needs to find someone with experience in the area to consult or with whom to mentor. In addition, there are often a number of "how-to" references that provide excellent legal overviews of various litigation areas. Or, call that favorite law professor and ask her to brainstorm with you concerning the law in the area. Though they may not be up on your jurisdiction's legal peculiarities, they can be very helpful in identifying new trends and new leanings on the cutting edge of various fields.

Of course the defendant can start with the complaint. What causes of action are proposed, and what does your legal research tell you about the ambiguity that exists in the law referred to in the complaint? Read the complaint carefully, even where you are not inclined to bring Rule 12(b)(6) motions. Any vague, boilerplate, or cookbook language in the complaint can signal areas of legal, if not factual, ambiguity.

In addition, there are a number of legal issues to get straight before proceeding to the witness interviewing. For example, if defending a corporation, does in-house counsel want to first conduct an internal investigation? Will such an investigation be privileged? Does the corporation want the litigator to promise confidentiality or job protection before conducting interviews with key employees? While these are factual issues, they involve the lawyer in doing some legal research and client counseling before heading off to do discovery. The procedural law, issues of representation, conflicts of interest issues, or confidentiality issues may each have to be determined before the lawyer proceeds to fact investigation.

While some lawyers start with the law and legal theory, there are many lawyers who feel that having a substantive legal theory early on in a case is of much lesser importance than having a factual theory. They argue that they later will find the law to fit the facts. Big firm commercial defense lawyers especially seem to send this message to their associates when they send them out to do fact investigation. The associates are often on their way before they have been given any idea for what they are looking. Part of this is simply the problem of senior lawyers who are "too busy" to take the time to be clear about their task or the delegated assignment. Associates and partners alike should aim for clarity before any assignment is given, whether the partners already know the likely applicable statutes or major cases in the area, or the partner or someone in the firm has previously written a motion for summary judgment or memorandum of law that covers some of the major issues in the case. What treatises or legal resources would the more experienced lawyer consult before they would head out to interview? Answering these questions greatly speeds the associates on their way.

Regardless of whether the law or the facts come first, at some point the litigator must return to law to get as close to a logical syllogism as possible. One very good source of major premises for syllogistic reasoning purposes can be found in likely jury instructions. For example, cases often turn on the credibility of witnesses, the weight the jury puts on expert opinions, the difference between direct and circumstantial evidence, or an understanding of the burden of proof. Consulting the model jury instructions at some time in the case analysis process can tune the litigator in to a number of follow up questions or areas of inquiry that she might otherwise miss.

In sum, whether it is because the client will need to understand and predict the likely outcome of a trial, or because there will finally be a trial, a litigator must develop legal theory(s) in order to provide good, sound, practical advice to his clients.

3.2 **Factual Theory**

Not only must the lawyer have a legal theory, she must also have a factual theory before the client can reach a decision about how the suit will be resolved. Certainly no later than the start of trial, facts and proof become paramount, but the pressure today is to have such theories in hand in order to determine whether to negotiate or mediate a solution. The factual theory is the means by which the lawyer will tell a cogent factual story that will persuade the opposition, or the trier of fact, that her client has an excellent chance of prevailing.

One might question the need for a factual theory before this time. Won't having a factual theory too early in a case blind the lawyer to contrary information, or suggest too strongly to the client and principal witnesses that the lawyer does not really want to know the truth about what happened, but only what fits his factual theory?

These are important concerns, primarily answered by knowing that at some point the lawyer will need a factual theory. Initially the lawyer's job is to find out what happened. Even so, the lawyer has to have some notion of for what he is looking. Otherwise, the lawyer's fact investigation is haphazard and inefficient. Just as scientist know the importance of having a tentative hypothesis to guide efficient learning, it is better to start a learning project having a tentative hypothesis than to go in like a blank slate. As long as the learner is careful to keep his factual theory **tentative**, he will be better able to learn what really happened than if he is without any preconceived notions of what to look for in discovery.

How should the lawyer initially decide on a tentative factual theory? There are a number of devices that can start the investigator on her way.

3.2.1 **Time lines**[2]

Early in a lawsuit, (maybe as early as before the client first leaves the office) the lawyer should try to sketch out a time line of the key events. For example a time line in a commercial case involving the purchase and coverage of an excess insurance policy might look like this:

---

2. I was first introduced to the use of time lines as a planning model by UCLA clinicians Dave Binder and Paul Bergman, in their book, *Fact Investigation* (1984).

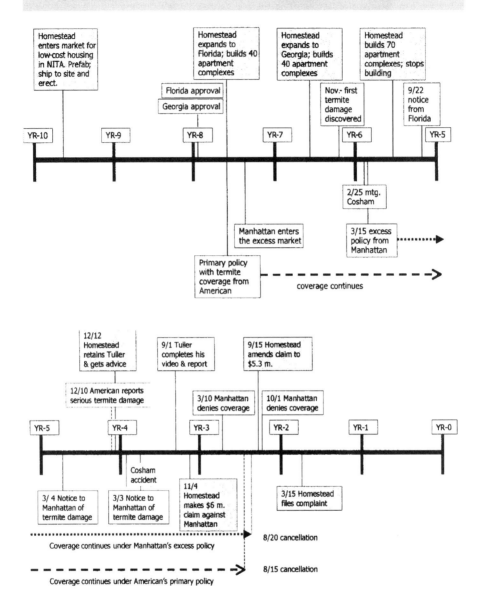

Look at the time line and start asking some questions. Is the first event listed really the first event that is relevant to the case? Often the litigator needs to back up the time line and ask what event(s) led up to the first listed event, giving the story listener a better sense of setting and context than what he has from the first event on the time line.

For example, in a standard car wreck, the time line often starts with where the cars left from on the day of the wreck. But as an earlier matter, what did the drivers have to eat or drink during their meals before the accident? What had they done the day or even days leading up to the accident? Regarding matters of credibility, who are these people and what virtues or character traits have they evidenced over the past years?

In an additional setting—in a commercial case, preceding the signing of the contract for insurance that may in dispute—what events led up to the signing? Was the contract a standard form, with boiler plate language, or was the disputed clause specially negotiated? If specially negotiated, what events required its special negotiation? Who contacted whom and why was the contact made? What events led up to buyer to need an excess liability policy? How did the buyer settle on the particular insurer? Why was insurer soliciting this buyer?

One of the greatest dangers then from using a time line is narrowing focus too much to the events immediately surrounding the dispute. Yet the time line stimulates a starting point for discovery and the lawyer can then structure his discovery to proceed chronologically. It is the way most of us learn. We learn by "starting" and then discovering what events followed.

Moving forward on the time line, a number of questions will immediately be raised. While you know that a meeting occurred, or an accident happened, you don't know what was going on in people's minds at the time they were acting. What were their motivations for meeting when and where they met? What communications, thoughts, ideas, feelings, and or emotions led up to those meetings? Why were they meeting at that point? Why were they on the road at that particular time of day?

In addition, the time line produces another set of questions. What **policies** or **procedures** govern the behavior at the time of the key events? Were there any notes taken at the key meetings? Was there a secretary present? Were the meetings recorded? Was a follow up memo or e-mail written? Do the parties keep telephone logs of their conversations? Do the individuals have standard ways of dealing with certain matters? If they do, how did they get trained about the procedures?

Another matter that the time line **will not show** is the things the parties did *not* do, people they did *not* call or talk to, or precautions they did *not* take. Moving down the time line, the litigator must start to look for key **nonevents**. These nonevents can be key to establishing negligence, especially where there are policies and procedures supposedly to protect against the nonevent happening.

Time lines are useful not because they answer questions, but because they cause the lawyer to focus and start to raise questions about what happened. Time lines are great for discovery planning because they force the litigator to look hard at the gaps between the key events in a known time line. They can spur the lawyer's curiosity in trying to discover the why and wherefore of the client's story, which can lead to all kinds of useful information.

3.2.2 **Story Outlines**[3]

A second discovery planning device that can be very useful to fact investigators involves imagining that they are about to have to perform the act of telling of a persuasive interesting story. Preparing a story outline can start the litigator on the path to becoming more imaginative and creative about what they might be looking for.

Ask yourself, for example, "What would I love to be able to say about the opposing party if I were free to make it up?" Imagining the darker side of a person's story can spur the imagination of fact investigators to look for those facts. It spurs questions such as: "I wonder if the other side's key witness ever got into any trouble? I wonder if they ever got caught lying or cheating or stealing? I

---

3. Binder and Bergman first introduced me to this planning model. NITA trial advocacy programs have picked up on this model and used it to help plan and organize a cross-examination. For example the cross-examiner might have a number of points to make during a cross-examination. Points on bias, lack of opportunity to observe, facts that the witness will agree tend to show the cross-examiners version of the evidence. One effective way to arrange these points of cross is to arrange them as a story teller might arrange them in the telling of that witness story. They might start with who the witness is, friend, foe, and their job as it relates to what they saw. It might then precede through the points chronologically, starting with the policies and procedures they usually operated under, then start with the facts they know consistent with the story presented in the order the cross-examiner wants to present, which pauses from time to time to point out to the listener what the witness did not do, as well as the witnesses motivations along the way, ending with the contact and interest that the witness developed and continues to develop with the opposition party in the case.

wonder if they are biased in any way? I wonder who they know and whether they are at all beholden to the people they know? What skeletons are in those witnesses' closets?"

In addition, the lawyer must be creative and imaginative about looking for good in their witnesses. What appealing things have they done with their lives? What social causes have they furthered, and what people have they helped?

The point is that human nature is often neither as objective and neutral, nor as evil and selfish as it seems. It is job of the lawyer to accentuate his witnesses' good sides and emphasize bad in the other's. This process is greatly aided by imaginative stereotyping and characterizing of both sides' witnesses.

Some experienced lawyers recommend that the litigator put down in writing brief, two or three paragraph story outlines both for the overall story that he might tell, and for the stories of the prospective witnesses. They then use these story outlines to seek out motivations, policies and procedures, and nonevents these story outlines might overlook.

3.3 Create A Cohesive Persuasive Story Outline

Another fact investigation planning device that many lawyers find particularly useful consists of asking, "What do I think really happened in the case?" Here the lawyer is using his or her own life experience to try to imagine motivations and reasoning and sort through the factual discrepancies of the case. Also, planning by asking what really happened can moderate the lawyer's overly aggressive tendencies and force the lawyer to empathize a bit more with the other side's witnesses.

For example, "Do I really think that the broker is lying when he says he thinks he told the insured that the policy did not cover termites? Or, "do I think that he probably had that in his mind, but forgot to specify it because he didn't want to do anything to put off the deal. Maybe he thought it would not ever come up?" Asking what most likely really happened will force the lawyer to confront the hard facts in the case—those facts which mitigate against the telling of the lawyer's most extreme factual theory in the case. In Homestead Properties Inc, for example, we do know that termites were likely on Addington's mind, because of Sedman's experience with termites. In addition, the fact that discovery has produced Cosham's notes, which corroborates that termites were discussed, (and shows no evidence of tampering), is a hard fact that speaks to Manhattan's good faith in its turning over of the document.

On the other hand, the fact that Manhattan never paid for termite damage as part of an excess coverage police is also a hard fact for the plaintiff to overcome. Should not the lawyer then, by asking what really happened, come up with a theory that it doesn't matter whether the party and nonparty witnesses lied, but that there is no expressed exclusion for termites? Ultimately what matters more is what Manhattan put in writing in the insurance contract with regard to the exception, to the exclusion for manufacturing defects.

In any event, creating a cohesive persuasive story outline can be very useful for spurring the imagination of the lawyer to look for key facts as the lawyer makes his way through the discovery process. In fact, what often happens in these story outline exercises is that the lawyer discovers he may be able to tell more than one story about why something happened the way that it did. Then his job is to pick the most persuasive story that he can tell. But why? Why need the lawyer tell only one persuasive story? Why not tell multiple persuasive stories and let the fact-finders take their pick?

Again, take for example the dispute about coverage of an excess insurance policy:

In such a case the insured is tempted to say that the broker promised to cover termites, the insurer promised to cover termites, or the parties did not explicitly agree, one way or the other, but the contract provides for coverage for termites. The problem with trying the case on all three theories at one time is threefold. First, the fact-finder often speculates quite correctly that you have talked to your client and indeed know what happened. Having multiple stories, then, the jury reacts like a parent or teacher might after hearing multiple versions of a story about what children were doing at the time something has gone wrong. With each version, the hearer starts to believe that they are not being told what really happened and when they hear inconsistencies they may question the speaker's character for truthfulness.

Of course, in criminal prosecutions, this may be all the defendant has left; that the state can't prove what happened. But fact-finders are often very keen to solve the case and discover what indeed happened. Multiple stories add to the cognitive dissonance of needing to solve the puzzle. If the defendant can relieve this dissonance by showing how the pieces fit consistently together, then so much the better. For plaintiffs and prosecutors this is vital. After all, multiple stories of what went on open up the plaintiffs and prosecutors to attacks that they don't know what happened, are speculating, and therefore fail in their burden of proof. The advice from most experienced trial lawyers is that if you do have multiple stories to tell, pick the best most likely one and tell it. Otherwise you risk the jury "seeing" through the multiple theory smoke screen that you are presenting.

3.3.1 **Law Office "Group Think"**

This advice can cause a great deal of cognitive dissonance for the lawyer. Which story should I tell? There are a few rules of thumb that many lawyers have found helpful in sorting through this problem. First, preview your stories before listeners you know who have good common sense. What you are looking for here is someone, not in your law office or particularly beholden to you, who can warn you away from the incredible, histrionic, or overly clever explanation for what happened. (While most good trial lawyers say "not someone in your office," many trial lawyers say that their secretaries serve this function for them.) Don't rely too much on what junior associates or even other experienced trial lawyers may think about your clever explanations. Law office "group think" can often overly encourage the lawyer to take the high risk of an overly attacking factual theory in a case. Instead it is better to think, "Can I sell this theory to Mom? Or a good friend, someone with good common sense?" Note, I'm not saying that you need to be able to sell your theory to a skeptic. You can control the atmosphere in the courtroom, or in a negotiation, so that the listener will find you sincere and likeable, and want to believe you. Yet your theory must pass the straight face test. Can you tell it with a straight face? Can you persuade someone with a foot in the real world?

As a fact investigating planning device, looking for one factual theory instead of trying to juggle multiple versions of what happened can also inspire greater efforts at finding out other facts consistent with the persuasive story you will tell in the end game. Another question a lawyer should always seek to answer is this, "If what I say is true, then what else would be true?"

3.4 Focus Groups for Early Case Analysis

Where case budgets merit it, another great way to refine your story lines and persuasive theories is by using focus groups early and often. The use of focus groups to pretry cases became commonplace in the 1990s. Some lawyers do it themselves, but others are enlisting the services of social science consultants to test-drive their cases with mock juries.

Early in the pretrial process focus groups can be used to determine what issues or questions jurors will likely have in response to your basic narrative of the case. These, in turn, can be used to direct discovery to answer those questions. Your goal is to determine the categories of facts the jury or ultimate fact-finder would need to hear about and the witnesses they would need to hear from. Just as in the brainstorming process described below, the goal of these focus groups is to ascertain likely first impressions of the facts and merits of a case in order to determine the values and beliefs associated with those first impressions. Once these have been identified, these values and beliefs can serve as guideposts for the litigation.

There are several methods that you can use to take advantage of what a focus group can teach you about the reception it is likely to receive from a fact-finder.[4] Each method has a number of common features.

1. the selecting of approximately a dozen people from a fair sampling of the community or a similar community from which the jury will eventually be selected;

2. members of the focus group should be paid for their time so that they remain committed to the process;

---

4. What follows is adapted from, Anthony J. Bocchino and Samuel H. Solomon, "What Juries Want to Hear: Methods for Developing Persuasive Case Theory," 67 Tenn. L. Rev. 543, (2001); These focus group techniques are more fully described in David Ball's, *How To Conduct Your Own Focus Groups* (NITA, 2001).

3. the convener should also have the focus group members sign confidentiality agreements covering all they learn during the process, as they will be significant participants in determining case theory and, at later junctures, in testing case theory;

4. the lawyer should arrange to contact the group members within a certain time period after the process, usually within ten days, to follow up with questions about the process;

5. the lawyer should be careful not to identify the party to the controversy that sponsored the focus group. Otherwise, the group members may respond in the way they think that party would want them to respond;

6. also, for that reason, the focus group sessions should not be held at the offices of an interested law firm.

At the beginning of the session you should ask the members of the focus group to provide you with basic demographic information: job status, marital status, children, where they live, level of education. Some who run focus groups feel that you should also survey the members for how they feel about the control they exercise over events in their lives. Samuel Solomon of Doar Communications, believes that this is one of the most revealing values tested. With respect to this particular value, people generally fall into two distinct categories: they either believe that events are within their control or that events are outside their control. Solomon believes that how in control people feel will impact virtually every decision they make about the meaning of facts and any conclusions to be drawn from them.

Once this and other relevant core values are identified, each group member is assigned a number; whenever a group member speaks, the member must identify himself or herself by that number. If you don't lead the session, it is important for you to be able to view the session without disturbing the communication between the leader and the focus group. One way is to set up a video camera with a feed to a remote room. Or, the entire session can be videotaped for later viewing (and/or transcribed if you would rather read what has been said, than listen to the video). These ground rules apply to all the focus group methods that follow.

1. The first focus group method is particularly helpful early in a case, to help direct the fact investigation that will follow. The session leader usually begins by describing what is known about the case in as neutral terms as possible. This presentation should include both the three best facts and the three worst facts as determined in the initial brainstorming session. You should then ask the group questions that seek their visceral reactions: "Is the plaintiff right?" "Is the defendant right?" "Is the plaintiff crazy?" After seeking a group response, you should follow up with individuals to explain their feelings. The leader's might then further follow up by asking the group members for any assumptions they might have made after hearing the basic facts of the matter. The assumptions can be about the facts of the case, the people involved, or anything else that occurs to them. In essence, the group is being asked, "If what I tell you is true, what else must be true?"

Key to this early focus group is for the leader to make specific inquiries regarding what information the group would like to find out and which people they would like to hear from before making a decision in the case. If the group asks questions that can be answered, the questions should be answered. If the leader does not know the answer to a question, the leader must communicate this to the group. Furthermore, the leader must honestly inform group members when the information requested does not exist and explain why it does not exist, if the reason is known (e.g., the plaintiff destroyed the papers). At the end of the session, the group members should vote for the party they believe should win the case and state their reasons for their votes. Approximately two weeks later, the group members should be contacted to gain any additional thoughts or insights they have about the case.

2. The second focus group method is more like feeding a fire by adding fuel a little at a time. You don't dump too much on the fire all at once, for fear of putting it out. It begins with the statement of several facts. After getting an initial response, the leader adds more facts, and seeks reactions from the group. The process continues with the leader unpacking the facts of the plaintiff's case and getting group members' reactions to the facts as well as their assumptions made from the facts. Throughout the feeding process, the leader should periodically allow the group members to ask questions and then provide accurate responses to their questions. By the end of the session, the leader should have unpacked all of the good and bad facts uncovered through the brainstorming session, and as a result of the group members' questions, should have determined other potential areas of inquiry through the process of the focus group's questioning. Again, at the end of the session, the group should vote on who wins based on the information available to them, as well as receive a follow-up call.

3. The third method is usually done later in the case. Its focus in on how to educate the jury about a legal or technical matter that is key to the outcome of the case. Often understanding of the jury instructions is vital to the outcome of the case. While this method works in any case it is particularly helpful in a case in which the jury will ultimately be required to apply the law and interpret facts that are outside the normal range of experience. For that reason, and unlike a negligence case based on fault, the judge's instructions gain heightened importance because jurors are more likely to listen carefully and apply the instructions with greater precision.

Not surprisingly then, this focus group method begins with the leader's presenting for the group, the elements of the claim or defense that must be proved at trial and that will be contained in the judge's instructions. Group members are first asked to react to the judge's charge by stating which of the elements is most important and why. The leader then makes a statement of the facts of the case, again containing at a minimum the three best and worst facts elicited during brainstorming. With this background, the group should respond to the question whether there have been sufficient facts to prove the elements required by the judge's instruction. From this point on, the session is much like that described in the first focus group method, where the group members ask the leader questions and identify information they would like to have and the people they would like to hear from before making the decisions required of them by the judge's instruction. At the end of the discussion the group is asked to reach a consensus. Each is then polled and asked to state their individual rationales for the decision. Some suggest it is good to follow up with a questionnaire. Others suggest a follow up phone call with in two weeks, in order for members to be able to reflect on the case on their own, and give a more thoughtful response.

By using any of these three methods or other similar methods, the lawyer uncovers those lines of inquiry that need to be followed through informal and formal discovery. Because the hot points for the jury are better known, both informal and formal discovery can be efficient, as the lawyer can direct discovery toward information likely to be persuasive for a fact-finder in the case. The focus group process also identifies witnesses from whom the fact-finder would like to hear at trial. In the rare case, the results of a focus group might even mitigate against filing the lawsuit at all, or at least against relying on a particular theory. And even for bench trials, there are organizations that can provide experienced, retired judges—with judicial records similar to that of the trial judge who will hear the case at hand—to participate in a focus group designed to identify facts and witnesses the trial judge will likely want to hear in the case.

Focus groups provide litigators with the information to be able, at an early stage in litigation, to identify relatively sophisticated factual theories of the case regarding what really happened and why. It may even be possible to reject potential factual theories because of the lack of positive response in focus group testing. In addition, the focus group process may also suggest legal theories of recovery and defense that are so problematic that they might be better off dropped from the lawsuit. At any rate, the information gathered from all the sources we describe in this article should prepare the lawyer to take the next steps in the lawsuit—steps guided by a well-informed fact investigation plan that is built on the solid foundation of what juries want to hear.

3.4.1 Brainstorming

The exercise of brainstorming can be very useful to both the end game story telling, whether it is at a negotiation or trial, and also earlier before interviewing or deposing key witnesses. Brainstorming is recommended by many creative problem solvers in business, science, education, government, and law. It is based on the notion that what unimaginative problem solvers often do is to too narrowly focus on a story or fact and miss the significance or the possibilities presented by connecting facts to other major facts.

One way to demonstrate problem solvers' tendency to narrow their focus too quickly is by taking a look at the following simple problem. Assume that you have been asked to solve the following problem: Connect the nine dots below using just four straight lines without your pen ever leaving the page.

Connect the nine dots below using just four straight lines without your pen ever leaving the page.

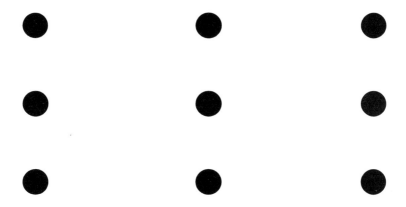

The problem is unsolvable if the problem solver sees the dots themselves as a boundary of operation. Now consider one solution shown below. Note that the key is to extend the lines out beyond the boundary created by the dots.

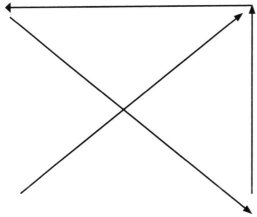

Other professions also struggle with a decision maker's tendency to narrow too quickly. Our medical and business colleagues have the same difficulties with misdiagnosis. Whether the tendency to narrow too early comes from a lack of planning time, or the impatience to wade through all the facts, or from a style of learning that is uncomfortable to that decision maker, (in Myers Briggs-terminology,[5] they may be a "judger" and have a low tolerance for the process of joint open thinking) there are obviously some real risks in recommending factual theories without engaging in some comprehensive thinking. One way of combating narrowing too quickly, and combating certain learning preferences that make it difficult for some to think more openly, is to engage in a step-by-step process called "brainstorming."

A system of brainstorming that has proven very useful to trial lawyers has seven parts to it, proceeding from listing "good facts" to "bad facts," "best facts" to "worst facts," "engaging in spin control," and the final step, that of selecting a "theme." We will take each step in order.

3.4.1.1 Good Facts

Set yourself up in a room where a group of your colleagues can also see a blackboard, whiteboard, or some common surface to record ideas. Designate a recorder. Then encourage members of the group to call out facts that in their mind are helpful to the case. Don't edit the ideas. Debate and ranking will come later. Now just get all the good facts out on the board.

One useful addition to this process is for the recorder to reflect back the idea to the proposer for two purposes. First, it is important that the recorder records the person's facts and not his interpretation of the facts. Second, the recorder should make sure he is recording facts and not inferences from those facts. For example, it would be incorrect at this stage to record as fact that Cosham assured Addington that Manhattan's policy covered termite infestations. Instead, the group should call out facts that support the inference that he made such assurances—that he wanted to sell the policy, that Addington was looking for this kind of coverage,

---

5. The Myers-Briggs Type Indicator (MBTI) personality assessment tool is a written instrument that "indicates" a person's likely psychological type. See Myers-Briggs.org.

and that Cosham's notes include the word termites with a double underline and question mark.

In addition, the recorder can be aware that he serves a very important function by making the brainstormer be precise with his facts. By being sensitive to the fact/inference distinction, the problem solver can be careful to be precise, and record for later reference from where the individual ideas are coming. In serving this role the recorder keeps wishful thinking from taking over the process. Many group planning sessions can be effected by a kind of "group tough" phenomenon where someone throws what may be a fact and the group latches on to it, and starts to plan as if that fact were proven. This was demonstrated in the recent auto products liability case where the defense latched onto a, "The plaintiff would have died anyway even if the gas tank had not exploded because he was dead at impact" theory. The problem was that no one had bothered to interview one of the eye witnesses to determine that the plaintiff was seen steering the pickup over the side of the road after impact. You can imagine their factual theory would not fly in the face of such a counter fact.

3.4.1.2 **Bad Facts**

In addition, or simultaneously, the group should also call out bad facts. The recorder can decide to try and hold all bad facts until after the good facts are exhausted, but often the group recognizes that some facts are both good and bad, depending on the spin one puts on them. For example, a recent startup's two years in the business can be good if it makes them the David against a Goliath, a multi conglomerate. It can be bad if it implies inexperience and inability on their part. Often recorders divide the board in half and record bad facts as well as good facts.

This process of calling out good and bad facts can take some time. If the history of the case is lengthy and somewhat complicated, the recorder might break the brainstorming process into segments according to a time line. This can be particularly helpful for getting the brainstormers to reflect more broadly on the early history of parties, damages issues, or "subsequent remedial measures" issues that they might otherwise miss. The recorder should be careful to hear from everyone in the room. Also, it is often in the waning moments that someone thinks of something "new" or missed, or tries out an idea that may give everyone a new perspective. Give time for the individuals to exhaust their ideas.

As the recorder looks back at the board, he or she should next encourage the group to look for connections. Are there groupings of facts that belong together? Are there connections that others had not seen before?

3.4.1.3 **Best Facts**

At this point the group should start to prioritize and focus on what is most important. One exercise has each brainstormer select the three facts he finds most important. Ask each person to write them down, and prepare to defend his choices. Then go around the room and have the individuals vote and briefly explain their vote. See if there is any consensus. Where there are differences, see whether through persuasion and discussion the parties can come to agree on what are the most important facts. Point out that these decisions will be very important for focusing their presentations of facts.

3.4.1.4 **Worst Facts**

The same process should be employed with regard to worst facts. This is important again so that the litigators don't prematurely disregard important bad facts that mitigate against their client's position. Next, the discussion should turn to the rules of evidence and motions in limine. Is there any way to keep out the bad facts? Is their any way of narrowing the focus of the dispute so that the bad facts become irrelevant?

Alternatively, is there now a need for more discovery? What counter facts are there to find? What additional facts may mitigate or overcome the otherwise bad facts? In other words, the Worst Facts brainstorming should involve a process very much like political spin control.

3.4.1.5 **Spin Control**

There are a number of spin control options persuaders should consider. One is to simply admit the bad fact. Perhaps a word of explanation is in order here. Remember the movie, *Clear and*

Present Danger, starring Harrison Ford as Jack Ryan, advisor to the president and all around good guy? The President has called his advisors to counsel him on what to tell the press regarding his connection to a man who was recently found murdered off the coast of Florida, in a boat filled with cocaine. Ryan comes late to the meeting, but just in time to hear some advice from an aide that the President deny that he even knows the man. We also see others advising the President to say as little as possible and saying "no comment." Ryan speaks up and advises that the President simply admit he was a very good friend of the man and felt terribly that he has died. In justification for his advice he says, in essence, if you admit simply, then what is to investigate? The matter will end there.

Similarly, where a witness or party simply, without excuse or apology, admits the bad fact and owns up to it, it can cause numerous salutary effects. The witness looks refreshingly honest. The audience is no longer curious about the matter and may leave it alone. If, however, the witness denies the fact, and it is later proven anyway, the matter has been made twice as bad. O.J. Simpson's argument that the picture of him in Bruno Magli shoes was a forgery is an example of how denial and accusation can be worse than admission that he used to own a pair of these shoes.

Of course another way to deal with a bad fact is to justify it or excuse it in some way. It is important, though, not to be too defensive. Referring to principles of primacy and recency, (that people remember best what they hear first and second best what they hear last, and remember less well what they hear in between) juxtaposing a bad fact with a best excuse, followed by a number of countervailing good facts, and placing the whole grouping about two-thirds of the way through your argument, can help de-emphasize the bad fact.

Also, you could deny that the bad fact happened, juxtaposing multiple facts and reasons why the bad fact could not have occurred. You compare witnesses for bias, documents for contradictions and omissions, and expert testimony for inconsistencies and overreaching. Again, if the client's case comes out weakly, persuaders can also make sure to use juxtaposition with stronger arguments to de-emphasize the weakness.

3.4.1.5.1 **Brainstorming The law**

While some may believe that focusing on the law too early can hamper creative use of facts, at some point it is necessary to also return to an examination of the law to look at the match between law and facts. Brainstorming techniques are also very useful regarding legal issues. When, for example, should a business client think about bankruptcy? When might it think about agreeing that plaintiffs be treated as a class for settlement purposes? Should the business client as a defendant ever think about the benefits of taking advantage of the multi-district litigation procedures? What about removal to federal court, or vice versa. How might conflicts rules and jurisdiction and venue options effect outcomes? Could preemption arguments help? Are there motions regarding the evidence that may be useful in helping to evaluate the case? Is a *Daubert* motion in order? Again, what do the jury instructions say about the legal issues in the case? Might any of the instructions be in play on appeal?

What about the law regarding the jury you are likely to get? Is there a need for a jury questionnaire, and on what issues? What is the receptivity of the court to various jury selection questions? How might court rules affect the probability that you get a receptive jury?

Brainstorming these legal issues can also lead to out of the box thinking that can better help the client reach their goals.

3.4.1.6 **Theme**

The subject of having a theme deserves separate treatment for a number of reasons. It may be the most important way to address what will really matter to the jury. Even if one doesn't engage in brainstorming, having a theme is vital to the lawyer's role as persuasive story teller. What do we mean by theme, and how does a lawyer "find" or create one?

Audiences make up their minds not only with reason and logic, but also from intuition and emotion. Aristotle described persuasion as the taking of a person to a place in the mind where he felt "at home." He called this aspect of decision making reliance on enthymemes. He described them as non rational bases of decision-making based on deeply held feelings, or on basic norms of fairness.[6] The world is too complex and the need for decision making too great for audiences to wait for "scientific proof" before they decide what to do. Persuaders have long known this. That is why they create themes for their speeches and try to persuade with an eye on feelings and the heart, as well as the head.

Two much-discussed recent lawsuits may help make the point. In the *O.J. Simpson* case the defense theme was "Rush to Judgment." The police were in a rush to judgment and they mishandled and planted evidence to reach a foregone conclusion. (A second theme also surfaced in the trial itself. This was the saying, "If it doesn't fit you must acquit.") The power of these themes was that they captured the underlying unfairness of the prosecution's case, made the defendant's points memorable, and hung the multiple parts of their legal theory together on something which was both catchy and gave the jury comfort that they were deciding the case fairly.

Another memorable example is a simple alliteration in the phrase, "King was in control." In the first *Rodney King* case, police officers were tried for beating the fleeing King and were found not guilty despite a video tape that showed officers pummeling King with their night sticks. Many of the jurors were later interviewed to determine why they reached their verdict. These jurors often quoted the defense lawyer's theme, "King was in control." Note that none of these jurors justified their decision with the words that the police officers were acting out of justification (self defense) in beating King for refusing to lie flat after being ordered to do so. They simply felt that it was fair to require King to lie down when ordered to do so, and that he was therefore in control of the situation.

A good theme that catches the attention of the jury, gives the client's case a feeling of unity, and speaks to the underlying unfairness or fairness of the client's case. The power of a carefully chosen theme is well documented. Whether by advertisers who make us remember their products when we go shopping, or politicians, who repeat their campaign slogans **ad nauseam**, or a preacher's

---

6. See Aristotle's Rhetoric.

sermons, or titles listed on billboards, the world is filled with persuaders who have thought about the power of a carefully chosen pitch or theme.

If lawyers agree that having a theme is important, they are of course only part way there. They must again find the particular theme that fits their case. Again, brainstorming techniques can be utilized. Everyone in your group calls out a catchy phrase, song title, biblical saying, or tries a little alliteration to try to capture appropriate theme. Another device many trial lawyers find useful is to try succinctly writing down an answer to the question, "Why is it fundamentally fair we win?" Forget the law for a minute, why is it fair or just that we prevail?

Often what happens in these sessions is the group refocuses on the best facts or worst facts in the case. Having a theme is sometimes as simple as noting an essential quote from a witness or a document. In the Homestead case, for example, it could be the use of the phrase in the contract "Perils Excluded, . . . this exclusion shall not apply to loss or damage resulting from such defective design or specifications, . . ." If the plain meaning of this provision is married with a defective termite specification, then Homestead's theme could be one of "broken promises," because it best sums up their position. Manhattan promised to insure it against a design defect, and now it is trying to take advantage of unstated customs in the insurance industry unknown to Homestead, to avoid living up to its promises.

One of the things that experienced lawyers tell us is that after awhile the cases they try play out on a number of recurring themes. They play out on issues of credibility of the witnesses, or the difference between direct and circumstantial evidence. They play out on the fairness or unfairness of holding someone to their burden of proof, despite the fact that someone has been injured. Other recurring themes for defendants in commercial litigation are that the plaintiff is playing some version of "the blame game"—**not taking responsibility for the choices they have made**. Looking back through the history of the dispute and noting the choices the plaintiff made that contributed to his own injury can help the defendant tie the case together under one unifying theme.

3.5 **Analogies**

The role of analogy or storytelling can help capture the theme and make it particularly memorable. One of the most interesting concerns in trial practice today is the use of analogies in making arguments to juries. Many trial lawyers question the persuasiveness of such analogies and fear risks in telling stories to juries. Further, many lawyers are uncertain both how to select good analogies and how best to tell the analogies they select.

In a teaching program, demonstrating closing arguments, Jim Jeans provided an instructive example of the use of an analogy. A wonderful trial advocate and trial teacher, Jeans, stood up to speak in defense of Dr. John Madden, a heart surgeon accused of committing malpractice during a heart transplant operation. The plaintiff had made out a very sympathetic case concerning children who lost their best friend, their father. The case against the doctor was largely circumstantial and depended, in large part, on the doctor's mental and physical condition going into the operation. The doctor had worked long days and gotten little sleep. In addition, the day before the operation the doctor's wife of many years had thrown him out of the house and told him she was filing for divorce.

Evidence from the autopsy showed that the suture had come apart at the point of connection of the new heart to the old artery. The actual suture, however, had been lost. Plaintiff claimed that the defendant surgeon either had nicked, cut, or burned the suture or had not tied the knot properly. (The plaintiff also sued the suture manufacturer claiming the suture was defective.) Plaintiff's lawyer, Dave Malone, finished his closing argument by emphasizing the loss to the widow and children.

Jeans then faced a hushed room, and told the following story. Speaking in a deep and controlled voice, he carried the audience back to "when I was a boy growing up in the Midwest in the 1930s." In summary, this is what he said:

> As a boy I rooted for the St. Louis Cardinals and was immersed in their baseball history. I was told many times of the year, it was 1926, that the Cardinals won the Pennant. The Cardinals then went on to challenge the

legendary New York Yankees for the world champion-
ship. The Yankees were supposed to sweep the series,
for they had an imposing lineup of hitters, excellent
fielders, and solid pitching. The Cardinals hung in
there, however, and managed to trail in the series,
just three games to two. For the sixth game the Cardinals went to their ace Grover Cleveland Alexander,
a tall pitcher, with a round house delivery. Alexander
was magnificent, and won the game. With the series
all even, the seventh and final game was set for the
next day.

Jeans then paused, moved and changed the pace and pitch of
his voice just slightly.

That night Alexander really celebrated. He stayed up
most of the night and in the process consumed a large
quantity of alcohol. After all, he expected that the next
day all he would have to do was watch. Rumor has
it that the next day Alexander was—if not drunk—at
the very least, still very badly hung over. With two
out in the seventh inning and with the bases load-
ed the manager called on him to preserve a narrow
lead and save the series for the Cardinals. Alexander
took off his warm-up and shuffled out to the mound.
Can't you just see it? He gathered himself together
and turned and faced the batter, Tony Lazuri, one of
the Yankees best ball players. He reared back, threw
a strike, and the crowd went wild. Grover Cleveland
Alexander then proceeded to throw two more strikes
to strike out Lazuri and end the inning. In the 8th and
9th innings, Grover Cleveland Alexander continued
to pitch flawlessly, throwing strike after strike until he
had struck out the side in each inning. He was magnificent, and saved the series for the Cardinals.

Jeans, after pausing to let the story sink in, argued that the issue
before the jury was Dr. Madden's performance, not his condition
before the operation. That like those fans who watched Alexander
pitch, the nurses and doctors who saw Dr. Madden perform the
surgery all saw a masterful performance. Jeans argued that no one
who saw Dr. Madden perform criticized his performance in the

operation. Jeans then proceeded to detail for the jury the evidence in support of his client.

There were many reasons to find Jeans' analogy persuasive. The imagery is memorable: the All American, tall, and triumphant baseball hero who helped the home team win the World Series. The point of the analogy is persuasive: professionals are trained to perform, and that at the time of their performance they are able to concentrate at a tremendous level, whether because of practice, adrenalin, their competitiveness, or their caring nature. It is consistent with the listeners' experience that there are people who, when the team needs them, step up, withstand the pressure, and do their best. Listeners also like a happy ending.

The analogy draws listeners to identify with the hero, and then the doctor. No one "directed" or "commanded" them, nor did Jeans constantly remind them he was a lawyer by "submitting" things to them or inviting them to consider such and such an argument. In other words, arguments made by the force of the lawyer's personality seldom go down very well, if at all. Jeans had framed the issue. Performance, not condition, was key to a verdict for the defendant. Also, and perhaps most importantly, the listeners now could identify emotionally with the defendant. Until closing argument many might have identified with the defendant only as an intellectual exercise. They knew that a defense for the doctor could be made on the basis that he was an expert heart surgeon, highly skilled, and technically proficient, but they had not thought much of the doctor as a human being and how to relate the doctor's fears and feelings to the jury.

Yet use of analogies presents some very real risks. For instance, analogies present dangerous possibilities for rebuttal. The opportunity presented to the plaintiff attorney in this case to twist the analogy around might cause some lawyers to hesitate in using analogies. The attorney for the plaintiff might have argued that Dr. Madden had not won the game, nor struck out the side, and no fans were cheering when Dr. Madden was through performing; instead, the doctor had thrown a bean ball and killed the plaintiff.

In addition, the analogy might invite the jury to put themselves in the shoes of the plaintiff's counsel, to make the arguments about how the doctor was not like the hero. The jurors could have easily become advocates against the doctor as they considered the analogy's weaknesses. The analogy might be fatally flawed in that it overstated the ability of anyone to judge the performance of the doctor. To illustrate, the witnesses had viewed the operation off and on and were only able to say that they hadn't seen the doctor make a mistake. One might ask whether, if a vendor in the stadium turned from a pretzel sale and saw a batter lying at home plate, and knew that the pitcher was hung over before he began to pitch, wouldn't the vendor be reasonable in concluding that "one must have gotten away from the pitcher?" If jurors start to make these types of arguments isn't it all over for the doctor?

Yet on balance, there are other reasons that tip the scale in favor of analogies. Jurors may be naturally sympathetic to the plaintiff anyway, and analogies gave the defendant a real chance at turning the sympathies around. *This analogy allowed the defendant to get emotional without getting emotional.* The characters in the story and intensity of the story provided the emotion. Real identification with the defendant's argument was possible. The story may make jurors really hear, for the first time, the traditional defendant's argument; that society needs its performers to be risk takers in order for communities to excel and become all that they were capable of becoming. The defendant doctor had finally been personified. Despite the fact that the defendant was evoking powerful emotions in the jury, the defendant's attorney did not need to become strident or defensive, but could remain reasonable, professional, and calm and examine the evidence in the light of his story.

Analogies are powerful. They tend to dominate the discussions after the closing arguments. To the extent that juries remember the story, it is also more likely that they will remember the point, and be persuaded by it. Analogies need to be used with care, especially where a responding attorney might turn the analogy around. An analogy needs to be edited with care, especially where it might overstate the storyteller's case, or over emotionalize it. Analogies standing alone (contrary to the impression left by the movie, *The Verdict*) seldom are persuasive. Had Jeans stopped speaking after telling the story, the jury would have felt that the story was an attempt to cover the arguer's lack of evidence. Analogies must be supported by enough detailed factual arguments to be truly persuasive.

An important side issue is also worth discussing. Analogies have to be examined with the particular sensitivities of the jurors in mind. If, for example, a Baptist preacher was on the jury who was sensitive to the use of strong drink as a way of celebrating, then Jean's analogy might be troublesome. Older women or certain foreign-born or first-generation people in the audience could be offended by the baseball analogy in that baseball is beyond their experience and is a typical male-oriented story. In this case, the baseball analogy probably is low risk because the non-baseball people can identify with the story either because they are baseball fans, or because they have had other team experiences that allowed them to appreciate the story.

3.5.1 A Caveat About Using Analogy

Finally, what about concerns over whether an individual lawyer has the skill to both select and tell a good story? Analogies might be rejected by a particular lawyer on the grounds that telling stories was not "his style;" that to tell the story would violate the advice given by many experienced trial lawyers that the key to successful argument was for the lawyer to "be yourself." Yet whether to use analogies is not a question of personality style. These lawyers are confusing questions of style with fears about how to select a story that they can both tell sincerely and that gets at the heart of their client's case.

Lawyers who hear the advice "be yourself," often interpret it in one of three negative ways. Many inexperienced and insecure lawyers say to themselves, "If I am myself. I'm sure to lose." Others take the "be yourself" advice as a way for the advisor to get out of telling the audience the secret of the speaker's success. Advisees have grumbled that the advisor seemed to be saying that either you had the talent to be a trial lawyer, or you didn't, and they guessed they did not.

Yet the "be yourself" advice, when offered in good faith and received in good faith, means something quite different and is crucial to understanding that using analogies is not a matter of personality type. The "be yourself" advice, for instance, certainly doesn't mean a trial lawyer can forgo finding and arguing the case law most applicable to their case. "Be yourself" means that the speaker needs to first discover the areas of concern shared by the court and the client, and find cases that allow this concern to come through. The lawyer then needs to organize his presentation so that the case authority is heard, understood, and believed.

Similarly, the advocate needs to first select an appropriate analogy. The attorney needs to put himself in the shoes of the client and consider both the rational syllogistic legal arguments that can be made and also consider the emotions shared by the client and the jury which are at the heart of the case. Once the case theory has been established, the world of stories becomes the lawyer's "case law of life." Whether the stories are taken from the traditional classics, folk literature, trial lawyer literature, or from personal experience, if the story speaks to the human condition in a deep and moving way, the story will help personify the client to the jury.

Once the appropriate story is selected, the teller needs to adopt the delivery which communicates their authentic caring position. At the heart of this process is the individual's ability to shed the images he has of what he is supposed to look like and sound like, in order that his natural caring and concern can come through. When a lawyer does this centering, the lawyer will use a voice tuned to be heard rather than to fill the space. The individual will care whether people listen and understand, and will critique their practice performances so that he will speak at a pace which people can listen to, and vary the pitch, pace, tone and volume, so that people can continue to listen to him. This is not a matter of personality type, it is a matter of communication fundamentals.

All trial lawyers can peel these layers of insincerity if they prepare well and think clearly about the strengths of the client's case. They can further help the process of "being themselves" if they can identify, in their own emotional makeup, with both the clients and the juror's emotional makeup.

In the process of selecting an analogy, then, the lawyer gets an excellent opportunity to think carefully about his theory of the case and also about the emotions in the case, both his client's and his own. The analogy then becomes a way for the lawyer to be himself for his clients. The experienced lawyer's advice does not forbid using analogies; it encourages authentic telling and individualized selection of analogies. The advocate gets a chance to show himself in selecting and telling the story. Telling the story allows the lawyer to show himself as a person with a history, with heros, and thereby identify himself more closely with the jury.

For example, the analogy Jeans used seemed to work both because it fit his theory of the case well and also because it fit him. It was authentic to the storyteller and was told authentically. For example, his apparent age seemed to make him old enough to have been around in the 1920s, in order to have seen the Yankees and Cardinals play in the World Series. The fact that he is a Midwesterner and lives on a farm, and the fact that he is a third generation Cardinal baseball fan, all help to make this story authentic to him. He could speak as an admiring baseball fan. He was able to identify, sincerely, with the human tendency to want to celebrate exuberantly after a victory. He also shared with the jury from personal experience that there are those people, when called, who repeatedly live up to people's highest expectations, even when they are given short notice. They perform particularly ably when the needs are the greatest. The story was also told sincerely, it wasn't hyped or overdone. It was spoken simply and clearly, with the story teller's pause for the introduction of a new subject or heightening of the natural drama of the story. While Jeans' story might not be for everyone, in every case, the way he told the story is for every trial lawyer.

While, admittedly, there is some art in telling a story, the art of telling a story can be learned; that with some practice and self critique, most any trial lawyer can tell a story competently. Remember how effectively most parents are in reading a story to their children? And think of the images this question invokes: the memory of a caring parent, in a warm, safe, and comfortable setting. The selection of the story, and fit between the story and the case are much more important to the telling of the story than the particular personality of the teller.

In watching different people read to children, it is easy to observe that the reader seemed to know with very little effort that if the reader is overly dramatic, too affected, is bored, or speaks too fast, the child will lose interest in the story. A reader's voice becomes warm and modulating when given a story to read to a child. Their voices warm naturally when they are describing things that they care about to people about whom they care. Fears about style often relate to self centered concerns that have been elevated over the speakers concern for the listener and the story. They typically pass as the teller gets into the story and is lost in the telling.

The benefits of analogies outweigh the risks, and most trial lawyers should be able to tell stories well. This does not mean that any analogy is good. There are certain pitfalls that need to be avoided. If the analogy teller uses a fact in the story that the jury knows is not true or that distracts the listener, for instance that the lawyer "was there," when he couldn't have been, or that the lawyer was the hero, the analogy doesn't work. If the listener feels misled, or feels that you are trying to distract him from the problem he has to solve, rather than helping him solve the problem, then the story does not work. If the story teller is obviously trying to be someone else the analogy doesn't work. Also, if there is nothing good that can be said on behalf of a client, then there is nothing to say in a story that will overcome this fact.

Assuming, however, that the case is at trial because there is real disagreement about what ought to be the fair resolution of the case, the client needs to be personified for the jury in order for the jury to really hear the client's side of the case. Analogies drawn from what the story teller really cares about, told authentically, and offered as a way of explaining a more difficult and subtle point because the teller wants to help the jury hear the story of the client, persuade more than dissuade. Whether or not to use analogies should not be the issue. The issue should be what analogies to use. When analogies are drawn from the lawyer's experience, are authentic to the lawyer in that the lawyer cares about the story, and tells the story sincerely, and when the lawyer is motivated to tell the story in order to truly help the jury see the plight of the lawyer's client, then as a tool for persuasion, analogies can't be beat.

Well, we have gone pretty far a field from fact investigation planning if we are talking about analogies. Aren't we getting ahead of ourselves? The answer is no, because without an idea of what to look for, lawyers will be less effective fact investigators and story tellers. A good fact investigator must both be open to "what's out there" and yet never lose sight of the end game. In the end, he will be a storyteller, persuader, and producer of a play, that will have a factual theory that fits and legal theory, **and** a theme. As Abraham

Lincoln purportedly said, "If I can free this case from technicalities and get it properly swung to the jury, I'll win it."

The role of focus groups in helping you determine the persuasive themes and their effect on likely jurors should not be understated. In fact, focus groups are often a great source of persuasive themes. Consider the *Dr. Kervorkian* cases.[7] In an early focus group, a elderly member is reported to have commented, "If we agree that it is okay to put a suffering animal to sleep, say an old dog, or a horse, shouldn't we at least consider it might be all right for people?" Such an analogy, or experience based decision, can then form the basis of jury voir dire, or jury questionnaires. It might help the lawyers better predict whether a case theme will resonate with an experience many jurors may share.

3.6 Graphics Help with Reverse Engineering

Finally, at some point in the fact investigation process the litigator needs to think about graphics. As with analogies, graphics can help you reverse engineer your case with your end game in mind. Think about how you might present your case on a single **anchor** exhibit. An anchor exhibit is a chart or board that you display throughout the trial to show or anchor the jury to your case theory, and why you should win. It should clearly and simply demonstrate the fairness of your case. It might be a key quote from an expert or opposing witness. It might be a graphic representation of the number of termite infestations that occur. It might be a computer simulation of the way the construction design of the homes led to the termite infestation.

The importance of creating a key graphic can't be over emphasized. The exercise forces the lawyer to focus their case into a concise clear representation that will teach their facts and tell their story. While good graphics can not overcome bad facts or a incoherent case theory, good graphics can go a long way toward teaching your good facts and making your best arguments about your bad facts, so that the opponent, mediator, judge and or jury, as the case may be, will understand your case. If attempted early, it will also help you decide what facts you should particularly look for, to make the visual complete and persuasive.

---

7. See "Death Becomes Him," by Jack Lessenberry, at http://kevork.org.vaniftyfa.htm.

It is vital for the lawyer to engage in case analysis to fulfill the dual roles the lawyer serves as both researcher/definer of the client's situation, and the shaper or creator of the story or narrative that needs to be told on the client's behalf. This narrative, with its component parts, legal theory, factual theory, and theme, will be necessary to persuasion not just at trial, but in a variety of strategic contexts; whether counseling the client, negotiating with the opponent, advocating the client's interests before a mediator. It will provide persuasive focus when speaking to the client about the client's case and flexibility to make quick decisions as more and more is learned about the facts. It also not only provides the basis to determine where other facts and theories may lie, but also to present an accurate and complete preview of the case to a focus group, to determine what may hinder a decision maker in understanding the case and seeing it from the client's point of view.

Case analysis helps forms an understanding of the client's BATNA (best alternative to a negotiated agreement), and is therefore in the background of informal dispute resolution all through the lawyer's handling of the case. Without an accurate comprehensive and creative case theory the lawyer's strategy is haphazard and random, and lets the legal procedure dictate case strategy, rather than provide the client with an understanding of the end game, and helping the client and lawyer decide the best steps to take to reach the client's goals.

❬•❭ ❬•❭ ❬•❭

FURTHER READING

Books

James Boyd White, *The Legal Imagination Studies in the Nature of Legal Thought and Expression,* (Boston: Little, Brown and Company, 1973).

Gary Bellows and Bea Moulton, *The Lawyering Process,* (Foundation Press, 1981)

Ruggero T. Aldisert, *Logic of Lawyers, A Guide to Clear Legal Thinking 3d,* (NITA, 1997)

David Mellinkoff, *The Language of Law,* (Boston, Little Brown & Co. 1963).

Aristotle, *Rhetoric*

Articles

Robert F. Hanley, *Brush Up Your Aristotle,* 12 LITIG. 39 No. 2, (Winter, 1986)

CHAPTER FOUR

LAWYER ROLES IN STRATEGIC DECISION MAKING: CLIENT COUNSELING

Evil counsel travels fast.—Sophocles (497–406/5 B.C.)

The client has a problem and comes to the lawyer, rather than the pastor, economist, or psychologist, presumably because the problem has a legal component to it. The question for the lawyer is what role the lawyer plays in helping the client solve his or her problem. The lawyer has a hand in designing a legal strategy the best serves the client's goals. As a preliminary matter, a lawyer needs to be clear about the lawyer's role with any client in helping him in decision making. How can the lawyer best help the client think strategically about where they are going and how best to achieve the client's goals?

There are a number of disciplines that can inform the client's involvement in forming legal strategy. **Moral Philosophy, ethics,** and **psychology** each contribute frameworks for helping to develop a strategy. In particular, moral philosophy provides a number of ethical models to assist the lawyer.[1]

> **Client-Centered Model:** The first and most prominent model is the client-centered model and is one based on client autonomy. It is the model imbedded in the American adversary system and the lawyer rules of professional responsibility.

---

1. Jacques P. Thiroux, *Ethics: Theory and Practice* (1977) (hereinafter Thiroux); See W. Frankena, ETHICS, 13-20 (1963); Professor MacCormick, who studies these categories in his article "On Legal Decisions and Their Consequences: From Dewey to Dworkin," defines this division of decision making ethics as follows:

> One can conceive of two extreme positions. On the one extreme, the only justification of a decision would be in terms of all its consequences, however remote B in terms, that is, of its productivity of the greatest net benefit, taking together all consequences and judging them by some suitable criterion of benefit and detriment. On the other extreme, the nature and quality of the decision, regardless of consequences however proximate, would be alone allowed as relevant to its justification or its rightness. MacCormick, "On Legal Decisions and their Consequences," 58 N.Y.U.L. REV. 239 (1983).

Delegation Model: A second model, a delegation model, is a variation of the first, but focuses on the delegation that can occur when a client asks a lawyer to be the client's surrogate in handling the client's legal problem. It is based on agency, or fiduciary contract law and is partially grounded in informed consent.

Social Psychology: A third discipline that helps to create a third model, the friendship model of lawyer-client decision making, is social psychology. Psychology, along with moral philosophy, explores the role that wisdom and care might play in the interplay between lawyer and client as they shape their legal strategy.

These three models are based on different paradigms, but are nonetheless, overlapping models that lawyers use in helping to strategize with their clients. Each has its own strengths and weaknesses. They are particularly useful to understanding lawyer counseling with an institutional or corporate client. These types of clients present their own unique challenges. Borrowing again, from moral philosophy, we use a principled approach to advising these clients. Such an approach uses expertise gained through experience in counseling institutions who have been in legal difficulties and from these experiences derives a set of principles or factors to help the lawyer protect the institution from the lawyer's own biases in forming strategy, and also guide against the client representative biases that can also skew the strategy. In terms of moral philosophy this model takes on the form of a rule utilitarian ethic. It lays out a set of rules and principles to guide the lawyer and institutional client in forming their legal strategy.

This chapter will describe each of the four models in more detail below and discuss their limitations.

4.1 The Client-Centered Approach

The client-centered approach assumes that the client sets the objectives or outcomes of the client's situation. It is based in moral philosophy that grounds the professional relationship between lawyer and client in the principle of autonomy. Autonomy of the individual is good because it promotes freedom, and freedom promotes experimentation and competition, and everyone is better off for it.

Under the client-centered approach, the lawyer's investigation of the situation is for the client's benefit, and it is unprofessional for the lawyer to manipulate either the factual or legal investigation, and presentation to the client to serve some societal or personal understanding of what the outcome should be.

4.1.1 Preliminary Observations—The Conflict in the Relationship

Consider the traditional view of the relationship between an attorney and client. Many clients take the attitude that it is "their" lawsuit and their business; that they ought to be in control. In order to be in control, clients need information that will allow them to reach informed decisions. Their need is for the lawyer to be an information retriever: "Find out what happened, and then analyze it and tell me what risks there are to my options." Even if the client has already done something illegal, he wants to be informed in order to decide how best to proceed. The client is not looking for moral approval from the lawyer. The client is looking for legal information about his options.

How should the lawyer take control of the situation when he has varying degrees of understanding what has happened? Even once the lawyer knows his legal theory, factual theory, and theme, how does he inform the client about the persuasiveness of their theory or theme, when its persuasiveness is in substantial doubt, or it depends to a great extent on the idiosyncrasies of the judge, jury, mediator, and negotiation opponent? Even where the lawyer knows enough about what happened, and what the law is, there is still a foundational conflict of interest. If the client has a need and right to control the choices that will have lingering effects on the life of his business, and if he has a right to run his business the way he sees fit, does the lawyer become an accessory to an illegal act where the client so chooses?

Herein lies the problem. Does the client have the right to control what risks he is willing to take, regardless of whether the law says he can take it? For example, what if Eleanor Addington, Homestead's chief financial officer said, "I admit Hirp explained to me that termites were not covered, but his notes don't back him up and I'll take my chances that in the end, insurance is for coverage. I want to sue."

4.1.1.1 Client Autonomy

Does client autonomy extend that far?

Taking this extreme idea, the client who is willing to engage in illegality, or at least walk over the line between truth and falsity to win, strongly demonstrates the conflict of interest that may exist between lawyer and client. Understanding this conflict should also shed light on the lesser, more usual, conflict between the lawyer's personal values and the non-illegal values of the client.

Before answering this question, it is necessary for practitioners to understand what might motivate the client to take this common, yet extreme, autonomy position. Many lawyers report that their clients pressure them to maximize returns at the worst possible time. For example, during deposition prep, or just before trial, clients will (and do) ask, "Who will know? Do we have to tell them? What if they don't ask? It's my life, and I'll decide."

Obviously, some of these clients may be responding to the panic and uncertainty of the moment. They are not necessarily thinking clearly and usefully about what is the right thing to do. They are running scared, and their fear must be dealt with by their attorney. Others are cold and calculating. They believe that litigation is a tool to get what they want and truth has little to do with it. Some take an amoral position to following the law. The law, or speaking the truth, is only one alternative that has no particular significance if breaking the law or lying would be more productive of the client's interests.

In addition, modern discovery rules may encourage clients to see litigation as a game. The discovery rules do not require that the sides volunteer their own weaknesses. The obligation is on the opposing lawyer to ask the right question or make the right discovery request. It is very easy for the client to get the message that litigation has little to do with what really happened, and instead has to do with "what is the best story we can tell and get away with it?" The client may rationalize that the other side must be hiding much because of all that he is hiding. The objections, motions, and tactics the client sees from the lawyers during the discovery process itself may help produce the extreme reaction.

Even when the client hasn't expressed the extreme position, the lawyer may assume, because of other pressures, that the client takes this position. The lawyer may feel pressure to do the spectacular, or magically make the bad fact, and bad case, go away. The pressure to maximize economic return to the client may initially come from the lawyer's altruistic desires to rescue their "poor client." In addition, winning is the most tangible measure of success for the litigator, and as the saying goes, "Winning is not everything, it is the only thing." If the lawyer wants to stand out above the crowd, even "winning" a majority of his cases may not be enough. After all, any lawyer can win a case where they have the facts. The really good lawyer wins when no one else could. To some lawyers, the best compliment that you can pay them is to say, "If I'm ever in real trouble, I want you on my side." The implication is the best lawyers get you off, even when you did it.

In any event, the lawyer's pressure to win may lead to false assumptions about the client's wishes and desires. This is one of the most common complaints about litigators: They **assume** that the client wants a no-holds-barred fight. If the fight ends up keeping clients from resolving their differences amicably and quickly, or once the client gets the bill and nets out the expenses, he may think more critically of the litigation tactics used and complain about his attorney, and all attorneys. In the language of economics, the client may have suddenly become "risk adverse." In non-economic terms, the client may simply view the risks to their other relationships as more important than strictly the economic return.

On the other hand, there are significant market pressures that do legitimately drive the litigator to push for one-sided, win-at-all-cost results. If a client settles a case, then finds out that he could have gotten more, or that other lawyers did better for a client in a similar situation, the litigator will often hear about it from the client. Personal injury lawyers are familiar with clients who compare what the lawyer says they should settle for with what the newspaper said someone else got. Also, the particular client may have high expectations. Some clients are "risk preferrors." They may be willing to risk more than is "rational" for a shot at the large gain. In other words, assuming a "zealous" representation posture may be partly driven by experience with a particular client's expectations and desires.

Many clients prefer to fight hard in the marketplace with all the tools at their disposal, or if defendants, to fight all comers in order to discourage others from filing suit. Their position may make sense if they are seeking to maximize their economic gain over the long run. To some clients, their legal position is a matter of judging the risks of getting caught in a particular mistake, as compared with the long-term costs of appearing weak.

The point is that the forces acting on the lawyer and the client during the counseling session are complex and partly inconsistent. In addition, when dealing with an institutional client, it could be that CEO wants one thing, the founder and chairman of the board another, and the shareholders, another. If the litigator **assumes** a particular motivation drives "the client," and gets it wrong, the client is very unhappy and feels that his autonomy and dignity have been violated. The real danger in counseling the client about what risks the institution ought to take is in failure to communicate clearly about what motivates the client, and describe comprehensively the potential consequences of the client's proposed behavior.

How can the litigator balance client autonomy and the need for attorney control, act ethically, and please the client?

4.2 Model Code and Model Rules

While the Model is clear under Canon 7 regarding the lawyer's obligation to represent the client's objectives zealously, it left to the Ethical Considerations the question of who controls what. EC 7-7 reads:

> In certain areas of legal representation not affecting the merits of the cause or substantially prejudicing the rights of a client, a lawyer is entitled to make decisions on his own. But otherwise, the authority to make decisions is exclusively that of the client, and if made within the framework of the law, such decisions are binding on his lawyer.

The same Ethical Consideration describes settlement offers, affirmative defenses, and pleas as examples of what the client controls. While not in the form of a Disciplinary Rule, the Code places the ultimate decision making power with the client. The Code's position is consistent with general agency principles that the agent must act in the best interests of the principal. Presumably the best interests of the principal are best determined by the principal herself.

The Model Rules clear up any potential ambiguity over whether the Ethical Consideration was meant to be mandatory with Rule 1.2 (a), which provides a new twist:

> (a) A Lawyer shall abide by a client's decisions concerning the objectives of representation, subject to paragraphs (c), (d) and (e) [(c) deals with the lawyer's ability to limit client's objectives after consent with consultation; (d) deals with the lawyer's inability to consult with regard to criminal or fraudulent activity; (e) deals with the lawyer's inability to assist the client with conduct in violation of rules of professional conduct or contrary to law] **and shall consult with the client as to the means by which they are to be pursued.** (Emphasis added.)

Model Rule 1.2 is remarkable for the obligation it places on the lawyer with regard to counseling, including selecting counseling means to be pursued. It forces the lawyer to consult with the client both as to ends and means, and subjects the lawyer to discipline for failing to do so.

Before getting to the **means** issue in litigation, the conflict within Model Rule 1.2 itself must be discussed. Model Rule 1.2 (d) provides the countervailing pressure:

> A lawyer shall not counsel a client to engage, or assist a client, in conduct that the lawyer knows is criminal or fraudulent, but a lawyer may discuss the legal consequences of any proposed course of conduct with a client, and may counsel or assist a client to make a good faith effort to determine the validity, scope, meaning or application of the law.

One of the most difficult aspects of 1.2(d) is defining "counseling" or "assisting." The lawyer is told that he can discuss the legal consequences of proposed courses of conduct, but that he can't counsel or assist the illegal conduct. How can a lawyer provide the client information without assisting him to commit an illegal act?

Comment 2 to the Model Rule gives only this guidance:

> A lawyer is required to give an honest opinion about the actual consequences that appear likely to result from a client's conduct. The fact that a client uses advice in a course of action that is criminal or fraudulent does not, of itself, make a lawyer a party to the course of action. However, a lawyer may not knowingly assist a client in criminal or fraudulent conduct. There is a critical distinction between presenting an analysis of legal aspects of questionable conduct, and recommending the **means** by which a crime or fraud might be committed with impunity. (Emphasis added.)

Apply Comment 2 to Eleanor Addington's situation. The lawyer might feel conflicted about whether to assist Homestead in its lawsuit against Manhattan. On the one hand, providing the client with an assessment of the chance of prevailing on the plain meaning of the contract surely seems necessary. Yet the lawyer may feel uncomfortable that by providing the information he is empowering the client. The lawyer is giving the client legal knowledge that he otherwise might fear was more than sufficient to argue against the illegal choice. He may be increasing the chances that the client will do the illegal act. Isn't giving information assisting the client in committing an illegal act? For instance, where a client may be contemplating murder and planning an escape, should he be able to find out what countries don't have extradition treaties with the United States?

While the comment tells the lawyer there is an important distinction between counseling and assisting, what exactly is it?

The issue for the lawyer is whether he must give the information that may increase the chances that his client will do the illegal thing. How does the lawyer make this decision? On the one hand, he can fall back on Binder's distinction between consequences and alternatives, and give up to the client the freedom to choose the illegal and fraudulent choice. On the other hand, he can refuse to give the information if he feels strongly that the law ought to be obeyed. And there is a third alternative. The lawyer could give the information, but engage in counseling to explore the morality of the decision. If the lawyer and client don't see eye to eye and the conflict would prohibit zealous representation by the lawyer, he can withdraw.

Under the second course of action, the lawyer insures that the client follows the law. The result is paramount to the lawyer. Consider, however, how the contemplated action may affect the consistency with which a lawyer decides not to give the client information that encourages illegality. Consider the often-given example of the client, a retail merchant, who is deciding whether to stay open on Sunday in violation of the county's "blue laws." The client wants to know what the fine amount is in order to determine whether to stay open on Sunday and risk the fine. In this instance, many lawyers opt for giving the information. If pressed, they admit that they favor doing away with the blue laws because it forces a particular religious observance on those who may not share the same religion. They favor "maximizing" client autonomy.

The implication, however, is that the lawyer is making his decision with reference to whether he agrees with the law. Where the decision criterion is whether the lawyer agrees with the law, he is saying something about his view of the law itself, and morality, and ethics, for that matter. And it reveals how the lawyer's view of different types of laws can lead to a willingness to subvert the law. The lawyer appeals to some higher law (whether an interpretation of the constitution, religious law, or natural law.) In any event, his view of the worth of the blue law is important to the resolution of one of lawyering's most difficult questions: "How should the lawyer counsel the client about ethical and moral choices?" Tell the client, and leave it to the client.

Assuming for a moment that lawyers share a distrust for certain types of law, the question becomes why they don't tell their clients about a general obligation to obey the law, and how law is necessary for orderly management of the community's affairs. The consequence on society of disobeying the law is not discussed, presumably because it is a matter of personal morality. On the other hand, where the lawyer feels the law is important to society, the lawyer denies the client the ability to make the personal moral choice.

There are further reasons why the lawyer may choose only between telling and leaving it to the client, or not telling and keeping the client from making the decision. After all, how exactly does a lawyer counsel someone about morality? The whys and wherefores of moral counseling are often left undiscussed for two major reasons. First, morality, values, and religion are all believed to be matters of personal choice and personal freedom. Second, there may be no shared language for discussion of value choice.

Some lawyers, however, do try to talk about morality on a basic level. Most situations of ethics and morality can be examined at the level of whether the decision maker is likely to be caught or found out, and thereafter pay in some way for his choice. The reference point assumes a personal egoist utilitarian ethic, balancing personal cost and personal gain. But what about other ethical systems of making moral choices? How are these systems to be discussed?

To determine whether to do "moral counseling," the lawyer must be clear on the nature of all counseling, whether legal, economic, psychological, or social. Once the lawyer has a clear model for other types of counseling, moral counseling shouldn't be much different or more difficult. As we shall see, it is often a matter of knowing what questions to ask, and how to draw the client into examining their decision comprehensively.

Whether the information is the lawyer's opinion (and should be kept to himself), or legal fact, is often beside the point. Where the lawyer and the client get out of step with each other is most often due to a conflict over values. The ethical dilemma is not trivial: it is most difficult where the lawyer's and client's fundamental values differ. The question is how do the lawyer and client communicate to each other about their different value systems?

The Model Rules and Code are clear that the client "owns" the lawsuit and the lawyer serves the client's objectives. One viewpoint on the lawyer's job requires the lawyer to be centered on the client's problem, rather than on self gains. The lawyer is an aid in solving the problem, not the problem solver by himself. Under this view, the problem solver needs to be client-centered in order for the counseling to be truly professional.

The first step in client-centered counseling is getting information. In this regard, dividing the skills of interviewing and counseling is somewhat artificial. Before any counseling can be done, the lawyer needs to be aware of all the relevant facts and feelings of both the client and himself. In addition, counseling will often lead to further interviewing, and further interviewing will often necessitate new or modified counseling.

Assuming, however, that the lawyer has gathered all the legally relevant information, there comes a time in the relationship where the information gathering stops and the lawyer and client turn their attention to problem solving. The Model Rules are the starting place for ethical problem solving through counseling. Model Rule 1.4 (b) requires that a lawyer explain a matter to the extent reasonably necessary to permit the client to make informed decisions regarding the representation. In order for the client to make the decision, the lawyer must give the client his reasonable options or alternatives, and then try to predict the various consequences from each alternative.[2]

---

2. In 1772, Benjamin Franklin described his problem-solving method—his "moral or prudential algebra"—as follows:

> When . . . difficult cases occur . . . they are difficult chiefly because while we have them under consideration all the reasons pro and con are not present to the mind at the same time; but sometimes one set present themselves, and at other times another, the first being out of sight. Hence the various purposes or inclinations that alternatively prevail, and the uncertainty that perplexes us. To get over this, my way is to divide half a sheet of paper by a line into two columns; writing over the one Pro and over the other Con. Then, during three or four days consideration, I put down under the different heads short hints of the different motives, that at different times, occur to me, for or against the measure. When I have thus got them all together in one view, I endeavor to estimate their respective weights; and where I find two, one on each side, that seem equal, I strike them both out . . . [A]nd thus proceeding I find at length where the balance lies; and, if after a day or two of further consideration, nothing new that is of importance occurs on either side, I come to a determination accordingly. Letter to Joseph Priestly in 1772, in 4 *The complete Works of Benjamin Franklin* 522 (J. Bigelow ed., 1887), quoted in Robin M. Hogarth, *Judgment and Choice* (2d ed. 1987).

To offer one alternative only is to substantially reduce the chances that the client will be the chooser. By analogy to the informed consent issue in medical malpractice, a doctor may be liable for battery when an operation is performed without making the patient aware of her treatment options and their side effects. Similarly, when faced with a series of choices (i.e. trial, negotiation, arbitration, mediation, or "drop the lawsuit"), simply presenting one option, going to trial, for instance, doesn't provide the client with the meaningful options to make an informed litigation decision.

Simply talking to the client in terms of options and alternatives, however, may not be ethically sufficient either. During the process of identifying options the lawyer may unconsciously take the decision away from the client. Imagine that the lawyer in a case involving a personal injury plaintiff leads off the counseling session as follows:

> Now, Ms. Addington, we could negotiate or we could go and try for a preliminary injunction. If you negotiate, you could save yourself a whole lot of grief and expense, not to mention the unpredictability of a court's decision about what and how to enjoin, and you will probably get close to what the court is likely to give you without all the expense of litigation. But if you want to litigate the case, I'm ready. It's your choice.

Clearly, the lawyer favors settlement. But what is wrong with him giving his opinion? Isn't that what the client is paying for? The problem is that in cases where the client, or client representative, may feel vulnerable, they may not understand what they are deciding. It's in these situations where the lawyer should be particularly careful to make sure the client both understands his options and makes the choice. Otherwise, the client may be very unhappy with the results, and turn on the lawyer at a later date.

Imagine, for instance, that Ms. Addington really wants a chance to tell the judge and market what a great product Homestead produces. She's got a litigation fund all ready built into her budget that covers her bills. What she wants is to make the defendants stop their behavior, and the market to learn of the decision, and she feels that litigation will bring about this result. Her true "values" conflict with the lawyer's assumptions about what motivates her lawsuit. Money is of lesser importance to her than principle.

But if the client disagrees with the lawyer, why don't they say so? The client may be intimidated, or may feel that the lawyer won't really try hard if he disagrees. Maybe he doesn't know they can disagree. Whatever the reason, the danger of the lawyer imposing his judgment on the client is significant.

Importantly, the danger can be easily avoided. With very little effort, the lawyer can make sure that the decision is the client's own, and avoid making incorrect assumptions. What follows is a series of suggestions for keeping the decision with the client:

1. Describe to the client the agenda for the counseling session. By describing the lawyer's role, the client will be less likely to read too much meaning into what the lawyer is saying. The lawyer can make this clear by saying, for instance:

> Ms. Addington, I thought we could spend some time getting clear about where you want to head from here. My experience has been that if we can fully explore your options and the consequences of each option, then you will feel more comfortable with the way the problem is resolved. What I suggest is that you and I identify your options, and then we brainstorm about which option is the best one.

2. Identify the options, ask if the client sees any others, and ask the client to choose which one they want to talk about. For instance, the lawyer might say:

> I see three options. We can proceed to a preliminary injunction, attempt some sort of negotiated solution, or perhaps find a mediator to help resolve the situation. Do you see any others? Okay, which one do you want to talk about?

By adopting the above as standard operating procedure, the lawyer can keep his own opinions from the client. Once the client accepts the fact he needs to make the decision, they can start to work at solving it. The client, however, may not buy the lawyer's agenda. He may not have the time or interest for making the decision, and may (and often do) ask "Well, what do you think I ought to do?"

A word of caution is important here. Before the lawyer jumps in and takes over the decision, he should recognize what motivates the question. Many people hate to make tough decisions. They would just as soon have someone else to blame. Or they don't like the stress of making a decision, or how they feel when they have to make one.

On the other hand, they may misunderstand, and perceive that the lawyer is trying to sell them something. They want information, and then they want to go back to the office, where they can make the decision in private, or with business associates and friends. In this case, the lawyer needs to be their partner, friend, and counselor, to whom they turn when they make tough decisions. The lawyer has both information and experience with helping people reach decisions. He is ideal to pick up pieces of misinformation, calm the over-emotional response, and help the client to look at the situation comprehensively.

Some clients, though fewer than most lawyers assume, are in control, for the most part, of their litigation problem and only want legal information. They only want the lawyer's frank input, and they will go away and make the decision on their own. Some like a good adversarial give-and-take to help them clarify their thinking. They want the lawyer to take a position against which they can argue. After the "fight" with the lawyer over what should be done, the client is more ready to make the decision. Once again, this kind of client is rare.

In any event, when the client does want the lawyer's opinion, it is important to find out why. Different levels of sophistication, behavioral preferences for making decisions, or different client values require different responses from the lawyer. If the client simply wants to put the decision off on the lawyer without taking ownership of their problem, then the lawyer may want to "make" the client work some first, before giving their opinion. If the client is strong willed, and simply wants the lawyer's opinion in order to judge the lawyer's bias in the information that will follow, then giving the opinion will not interfere with taking ownership of the decision.

One option for dealing with the client's expectation is for the lawyer to give his opinion, but explain how it may be biased. This option falls in the general advice category "if in doubt, honesty isn't a bad place to start." For instance, the lawyer might say:

> Ms. Addington, if it were my problem, I'd first try to get a realistic estimate of the cost of doing nothing, ignoring this problem. I would want to know all the adverse effects on the business, and the people involved in the business, if management just walks away. Any effort to resolve this problem, whether by settlement or through the legal system, will take time and effort of key managers and investment dollars that would otherwise be devoted to the business. After I figured that out, I would try to reach a settlement. But you need to understand that I'm looking at this partly from time savings versus dollar return to me. I'm wondering whether the increased hearing preparation time will produce a sufficiently greater return at the hearing than what we can get now. On the other hand, only you know what you are trying to get out of this. So let's consider my opinion for what it is, just my opinion, and talk about what is likely to happen, assuming you pick various alternatives. After all, it's your decision to live with, not mine, and my job is to work as hard as I can to see you get what you want.

3. Identify areas where the client has superior information about the effects of the various decisions. Binder, Bergman, and Price, in their book *Lawyer as Counselor*, suggest that lawyers look for categories of information about which the client has superior information.[3] While the lawyer has the superior information base about the law and the legal setting, the client usually has superior knowledge about the economic, social, psychological, and moral/religious effects of the decision.

Binder et al. suggest a prepared chart for that purpose with alternatives running along the side, and legal, economic, and social/other factors running across the top. Whether you develop, chart, and write down things that the client says in the appropriate box, or simply ensure that each factor is discussed, is a matter of interviewing preference. What is essential is for the lawyer to see that the economic impact of the decision is something about which the client usually has much better information.

4.3 Predicting Social, Psychological, and Moral Consequences

In some ways the counseling about the law and the likely outcome in terms of a jury verdict (or BATMA [best alternative to a mutual agreement]) is the easy part. What can get the lawyer cross ways with the client fastest, is for the lawyer to misread and make wrong assumptions about the client's social relationships, psychological needs, or moral and value interests.

Even the economic consequences of a particular outcome have client specific features to them.

While the lawyer may be able to predict the dollar value of the litigation, usually only the client knows the cash-flow effect, how the litigation affects other sources of income he might have, what the tax effect will be, or how money spent on litigation affects other opportunities the client may have. The client may, however, be seeking economic information. The client may want to know what the jury will award, or what the judge will order by way of a fine. The lawyer, in this case, is giving quasi legal advice, which depends for its legitimacy on the lawyer's experience in similar matters, or information sources that help predict the economic consequences.

---

3. Paul A. Binder, Paul Bergman, and Susan C. Price, *Lawyers as Counselors: A Client-Centered Approach*, 83 (West, 1991)

Binder and Price point out, given this economic and legal information, that the client often already possesses superior information concerning the economic consequences of various choices. The client may know better what an order granting him child custody will cost in the way of expenses. Or, the client may know how a product recall will affect his company's bottom line. For the lawyer to assume he has greater information about economic consequences can lead to embarrassing and bad advice.

The lawyer is not without a role, however. The lawyer's job in this area is to clarify the client's thinking about the economic consequences. The client may not be thinking comprehensively about the problem. The client's emotions or preoccupation with one aspect of the problem may cause him to lose sight of the big picture. The lawyer should look out for this possibility, and if he is surprised by the outcome, or finds some of the client's reasoning inappropriate and irrational, he should seek to clarify the client's understanding of the problem.

It is important at this stage for the lawyer to be clear with the client about what the lawyer is doing. Without an explanation of the lawyer's clarifying role, the client could take the lawyer's questions as disagreement with the client's choice. If Ms. Addington says "I never want to settle," and the lawyer responds "Why do you say that?" Ms. Addington may "hear" that her lawyer disagrees with her statement. To protect against being misunderstood, the lawyer must first describe his questioning role, and ask the client to clarify her reasoning in order to help the client to be careful and comprehensive in his thinking. The lawyer can ask questions, for example, "Won't an agreement between you and Best Homes send an effective message to the market about the quality of your product? What kind of an agreement might do that short of a trial? What is the value of an apology? What if it were public? In other words, "Is your picture of settlements too narrowly drawn?"

4. Ask how the client feels about an option, as well as what he thinks about it. Often what drives an initial emotional, passionate decision to litigate is a fear of the economic effect of the opposition's behavior. Depending on whether that economic impact is actualized, the passion for the litigation may either increase (where the economic situation becomes more desperate), or decrease (where the supposed costs of the opposition's behavior never materialize, or other opportunities make the significance of litigation diminish.) The client's emotional feelings are key to understanding his position.

In addition, the lawyer must realize that the client bears the primary social, psychological, and even moral or religious effects of the litigation. After all, it is the client who must live with having sued and received nothing, or having settled for a promise that has little enforceability and which means little if the market has already been misinformed. Just as it is the client who must decide whether spousal support should be higher, or whether child support should be higher, and risk a custody fight, so the business client must decide whether to fight or take less than their legal right. Each of these decisions affects the business's place in the market, as well as the client's short term economic welfare. Asking how each option will affect their significant relationships, customers, competitors, bankers, capital venturers, and shareholders, will clarify these other concerns for the client.

In addition, we come full circle to the earlier issue of counseling about morality issues. But now we should have a model in place for discussing these topics. The lawyer should gain access to this information by asking how the client feels about his decisions, as well as how he thinks about them. This will produce a jumble of social, psychological, and moral reasoning. This reasoning needs to be clarified for the benefit of the client, so that he understands the effects of his choices, and comes to "know" what is right for him to do. Just as the medical profession needs to respect the religious patient who doesn't want a blood transfusion and sets up procedures to identify these patients, lawyers should be on the look out for feelings, beliefs, and attitudes that change the set of solutions that are available to their clients.

It would be wrong for the lawyer to think that he brings no information to the counseling session on social, moral, and psychological issues. The lawyer, as he practices law, should be learning from experience the effects that client's decisions have on their later level of satisfaction. The lawyer should be able to offer advice based on what he has experienced or been told of the reaction clients may have to trying, dropping, or settling cases. In fact, referring to this experience, or referring to what the lawyer has been told, is key to raising some of the important social and moral issues and helping clients to clarify their thinking. The lawyer might say:

> My experience has been (or, in discussions with other legal counselors, I've heard) that some clients wished that they hadn't gone ahead with a hearing. They feel that taking the witness stand made them destroy all chances to reconcile with the other side. They now wish they had sought a business settlement. How do you think you would feel if you did win at the hearing? Would there be any costs to your future relationship with the other side that you would be worried about?

To borrow from the language of decision-making theory, the lawyer *facilitates* the client's decision by getting the client to imagine that they have made each decision and are living with the consequences. Part of this technique is to ask the client to assume the role or character of the different persons who will be affected by the client's decision. The lawyer thereby teaches the client "advanced empathy" or emotional intelligence. The counselor enables the client to "try on" the decision, to see if it feels right and fits from different perspectives.

Binder and Price suggest that the lawyer see his role as both giving and clarifying information. The lawyer's purpose is not to manipulate the client to reach the decision the lawyer thinks is right for the client. The lawyer primarily gives information about the legal consequences of the client's various choices, but also helps the client clarify his own values in order to increase chances that he will get maximum satisfaction for his decision.

There are, however a number of problems that develop when lawyers use the client-centered model. These are not necessary problems with the model but they are brought about by the unreflective and rote use of any allegedly objective and neutral informed consent model. A description of some of the more obvious problems that may develop follows.

4.4 **The Problem of Lawyer Low Balling**

The lawyer must be careful neither to "low ball" the client nor overvalue the client's legal position. Of the two potential problems, low balling is the more common ethical pitfall. "Low balling" refers to some lawyers' practice of telling clients that their chances of success in court are very low, in order to please the client when the lawyer reaches a negotiated settlement of more than what he initially said the case was worth. The negotiated settlement makes the lawyer look like a tough bargainer, and the client is thankful and surprised by the amount of settlement. The lawyer guards against the possibility of valuing the case too optimistically, which may result in the client being disappointed and the lawyer looking like he failed. To protect against client disappointment, some lawyers low ball.

Low balling denies the client the ability to make his own decision about the lawsuit. The lawyer has, in effect, made the decision for the client. Without an accurate assessment of the legal status of the case, the client may be too willing to settle, and decide to settle too low. The client's decision to settle is not informed.

On the other hand, if the lawyer gives the client too rosy a picture, the lawyer is unable to reach agreement lower that the one promised, because the lawyer's earlier promises make the lawyer too wedded to the rosier outcome. Some plaintiff's lawyers, in particular, find themselves unable to step back from their clients case during the heat of the negotiation, and objectively assess the weaknesses as well as the strengths of the case. The lawyer's job, then, is to be neither too hot nor too cold, but get the valuation questions "just right."

4.5 **Giving The Client The Bad News**

Another ethical problem can arise because the litigator doesn't want to be the bearer of bad news. In fact, this is likely with a client like Ms. Addington. After all, Homestead may indeed build poor quality homes. Imagine that Homestead had been dissatisfied with its other law firm. Perhaps the old law firm thought the client should drop the law suit and simply do a better job competing in the market place. Their recommendation led to Homestead wanting to switch firms. Now, it looks like the old firm's evaluation of the lawsuit was about right. How does the lawyer deliver this "bad news" without losing the client?

The lawyer may be severely tempted to let the lawsuit run its course, so that the bad news comes from the court and jury rather than from the lawyer. And, despite the well-known advice to the contrary, sometimes people **do** kill the messenger. Once again, the lawyer needs to understand that the client has a right to the information so they can make an informed choice. The skillful counselor should be able to give the information in a way that doesn't risk the relationship. To do this, the lawyer needs to make sure that the client understands that litigation is the client's choice, brought about by the client's actions, with a number of perhaps unintended consequences. The client needs to see the lawyer as a counselor, not the judge. The lawyer can make these roles clear by describing the counseling process and by taking care with his language. He needs to be careful to both develop his language of prediction, and transfer any value judgments to be made onto the backs of the true decision makers. For instance, the lawyer might say:

> Ms. Addington, I would predict three likely outcomes at a preliminary injunction. First, and this in my judgment is most likely, the judge could decide that a preliminary injunction is not warranted because of the court's (1) uncertainty about the free speech aspects of an injunction—a prior restraint on speech—(2) and uncertainty about the nature of your product, and (3) the little evidence we have that what Best Homes has done comes from Best, or (4) that it has affected your sales adversely. I would estimate our cost for gearing up in the short term would be about $140,000. On the other hand, if we can convince the court that though your sales have been good, they would have been even better without the behavior of Best Homes, and that you have been injured or are likely to be severely and irreparably injured, then the court might enjoin them from making false statements in the future. As the case stands right now, I'd say we don't really have the goods on that, and it would depend on how both you and our expert would do in front of

the court. Finally, there is a chance that the judge could side completely with Best Homes, and decide that your product is not of high quality, and that is a decision you certainly do not want public. I'd say the chances of the first result are about 60 percent, and the chances of the second two are about 20 percent each.

Of course, some lawyers would be uncomfortable putting percentages on the outcome. They might prefer to talk in terms of "most likely" and "least likely" results. While percentages fine tune the client's understanding, in either case, the client has been given the lawyer's frank opinion about what will happen at trial so that the client can decide what risks he wants to take.

The language of prediction is also related to the jury's role in the decision. The lawyer remains neutral. In addition, the lawyer is not attacking the client's product or values, but the opposition is. It is the opposing attorney who is calling Homestead's product inferior. The client is thereafter drawn into a discussion of the lawyer's reasoning and prediction process, and is given the chance to understand the lawyer's calculations of the outcome at the preliminary injunction.

The lawyer's goal need not be to bring to the client a total understanding of his reasoning. After all, part of the reasoning process is three years of legal education and more years of practice experience. Yet the client is entitled to substantial understanding of the forces that go into the lawyer's opinion. Just as the patient should be encouraged to inquire into why the doctor is recommending an option, the client should have the same opportunity to inquire of the lawyer. The patient doesn't need to know exactly the basis of the doctor's "percentage of recovery" opinion, whether based on epidemiological studies or on some other basis. The client doesn't need to know, either, unless he asks whether the jury prediction comes from a comparison of similar cases, or from jury verdict research, or from the attorney's intuition. The client, or client offeror representative, does need to have some information about where the lawyer predicts the case will end up and why. That is what the client is paying for.

4.6 Taking Ethical Control of The Case in A Client-Centered Approach

While we have discussed certain philosophical arguments about the difficulties of counseling a client who wants to do something illegal, the lawyer must understand the particular risks of counseling or assisting a client to commit perjury. At the risk of stating the obvious, if the Model Rules won't get you, malpractice and criminal actions will. Recent litigation demonstrates that when clients get caught doing something illegal, one option is for them to blame their lawyers for advising them that it was okay to do so. The files are opened, and the client tries to prove his lawyer was to blame. The risk to the lawyer is real and great: his license can hang in the balance.

If the client's values have been clarified to the extent that they express a willingness to do whatever is necessary to win, then the lawyer ought to have no hesitation in taking control. The lawyer doesn't need to be angry or "holier than thou," just clear. He can start with self-interest appeals, move to altruistic appeals, and finally make threats, as ways of persuading the client. The lawyer might say:

> Ms. Addington, are you saying that you would be willing to lie or ask your accountant to lie to win the lawsuit? Ms. Addington, I need to be clear with you about this from here on out. You don't want to commit perjury. Not only is it my experience that the court will know, and that the other side will make you pay during their cross-examination, but you risk a criminal prosecution. You risk your reputation, and your good standing in the community.

[If this doesn't bring ready agreement from the client]:

> In addition, Ms. Addington, you surely don't want to unfairly deny to Best Homes an ability to compete in the market place.

[If this doesn't do it]

> Ms. Addington, I risk losing my license if I put either of you on the stand when I know you are going to

lie. While your case is important, I'm sure you understand that I have other obligations, like continued
employment and reputation, that I have to consider.
If you insist on taking the stand and lying, I have to
withdraw right now.

The Model Rules and Code each provide that the lawyer must
take ethical control of the litigation to protect the integrity of the
process. Model Rule 3.4 (b) reads:

A lawyer shall not:

(b) falsify evidence, counsel or assist a witness to testify falsely, or offer an inducement to witness that is
prohibited by law;

DR 7-102 (A)(6) reads,

(6) a lawyer shall not participate in the creation
or preservation of evidence when he knows or it is
obvious that the evidence is false.

The Code and Model Rules raise the obligation to withdraw
before suborning perjury.

The problem is that lawsuits have bad facts in them. Each side
has them. That is often why there is a lawsuit in the first place.
The lawyer's job is to characterize and argue zealously about the
meaning of their client's facts. But they must take control and draw
the line at the creation of new facts.

4.6.1 The Client May Want More from The Lawyer

In addition, there is a greater and greater cry from the client
that the lawyer be more than just a neutral information provider
and warrior for the client.[4] The client may want the lawyer to actually care about whether the client is doing the "right" thing. The
client may want "wisdom" from the lawyer. After all, the lawyer
presumably has experience with clients who have been in similar

---

4. I have written elsewhere in criticism of the prevailing model. See Hamric and
Zwier, "The Ethics of Care and Reimagining the Lawyer/Client Relationship," 22 J.
CONTEMP. L. 383, (1996).

situations. How did these clients feel after their suits? Were these clients' victories hollow? Did they win the battle but lose the war? Did they win the lawsuit but lose market share? Did they win short-term market share, but lose customer loyalty? In the case of Ms. Addington, did they prosecute successfully the lawsuit only to raise unrealistic expectations in their customers?

Many clients want their lawyers to care about these questions. They want to be engaged in a conversation with a person who really understands their business and can speak wisely and forcefully about the choices that matter most to the client. They want a lawyer who shares with them a different model for their working relationship.

1. Interviewing and Counseling are necessary to determine the client's goals. Listening Skills are also important as a foundation to the problem solving that follows.

- What are the salient factual issues?

- What losses have been suffered and what caused these losses?

- What is the market for Homestead's Homes?

- What is the market for Best's Homes?

- What are Eleanor Addington's goals and ambitions?

- What is Homestead's mission statement and strategic plan?

- What are the Steadman's goals and ambitions?

- What are the key figures in the business? Suppliers, marketers, investors?

2. Identify alternatives

- Litigation for injunction

- Litigation for law suit

- Mediation

- Negotiation

- Client to client

- Lawyer to lawyer

3. Predicting consequences

- Costs to the business

- Time of key personnel

- Legal fees

- Market forces

- social

- psychological

One practical way to help the lawyer implement a client-centered approach in a client counseling session is for the lawyer to prepare a counseling chart. A counseling chart can help the lawyer show the client where the client needs to give input, and where the tension lies in reaching a strategy. The chart can lay out the alternatives and consequences and provide space for client input on creative alternatives and client weighing of competing considerations to help clarify for the client the choices the client needs to make.

One example of client-centered counseling chart would look like the following: Counseling Chart for Homestead, Part I. (Homestead tells the lawyer that A-Best, a competitor is disparaging them in the market place by telling customers that Homestead's housing is poorly made and termite infested. What strategy should be employed?)

Counseling Chart

↻ ⇨	Preliminary Injunction	Party-to-Party Negotiation	Lawyer-to-Lawyer Negotiation	Mediator
Legal Consequences	Expensive unlikely winner	Covenant not to compete violates unfair competition? Common law? State and Federal anti trust?	Covenant not to compete violates unfair competition? Common law? State and Federal anti trust?	??
Business Consequences Competitors Suppliers Bankers Shareholders				
Social/ Psychological Consequences				
Moral Consequences				

This chart can help to get the client and lawyer, literally on the same page about what is to be done and why. It can also provide great information to help in the lawyer's implementation of the client's choices through the negotiation and mediation of the case.

4.7 Lawyer as Surrogate Decision Maker

A second model for lawyer-client decision making is for the client to simply delegate to the lawyer the power to make decisions for him, "in his best interests." Consider the very reasonable position that clients simply don't want to know or worry about the litigation. "You, the lawyer, are getting paid a lot of money to handle my legal matters. I have other things to worry about. You make the decisions that arise out of the legal issues and just keep me informed as we go along. I'll pay you to do my worrying, and I'll get some sleep tonight."

This kind of relationship is not uncommon. It can arise in the federal regulatory area, where clients simply want the government to interfere with their business as little as possible. They hire lawyers who will fight to get the EPA, SEC, or FTC off their backs. The client has been accused of violating some regulation and the client wants the lawyer to make it go away.

The surrogate model can affect, dramatically, what information you present the client and whether one of the lawyer's legitimate concerns is protecting the client from knowing too much. This kind of relationship, however, runs some real risks. Its exact nature needs to be well documented. Even then, when particular issues arise that strike at the very heart of the client's needs, the lawyer must be careful that he is up to date on the client's best interests. To the extent that their interests in the marketplace may change, or the client's method and persona may have to vary, depending on the particular person they are dealing with, the lawyer runs the risk of getting away from the delegated authority they presume they have.

Other risks in this kind of relationship include:

1. Accentuating the game of hiding information. Clients may also see it is to their advantage to have an advocate who does not know what has really gone on. Such knowledge of the "bad" facts or sloppy management may affect the lawyer's willingness to fight vigorously for the client. Not telling all to the lawyers also protects the lawyers from knowing that they are lying when they are asked questions by the government about what the client knows, or is doing, or has done. These situations are analogous to the criminal defense lawyer who starts off his interview with his client by saying, "I don't want to know what happened, I just want to know what story you want me to tell."

2. May make it difficult to investigate internally. Many lawyers who are treated as surrogate warriors (like the old English Barrister model, where the lawyer has little direct contact with the client, but are fed information they need about the case through a solicitor, on a need to know basis) report that they have a hard time getting information from the client about who knows what and when they knew it. Their relationship with in-house counsel is crucial. In-house counsel feeds the litigator what they need, and can closely control the lawyer's access to information.

3. Lawyer may be seen as a warrior who fights more for self than for the client. Again, there is logic to the delegation/surrogate model that comes from basic contract law and models of fiduciary relationships that exist when any officer acts on behalf of an institution. The client might think that the client is delegate the fighting job to the litigator. The client could rightfully believe that he gets **wise** counsel from in-house counsel. The CEO may have also done the business calculation and determined that it is better to fight than build relationships. The management may believe that it is always better to fight aggressively in "these kinds of cases" so that they have a policy in place that does not need to be rethought each time they are involved in litigation. Yet the unintended effect on the lawyer-client relationship can be profound. The lawyer can believe that their continued success with the client is to win at all costs. He may not have been privy to the thinking behind the policy to fight and therefore assume that their clients are amoral at best, and affirmatively a sociopath, at worst. This can lead the partner or associate to not understand or respect the client's thinking, which can in turn lead to an undue focus on winning. After a while, it may be hard to get sufficient meaning and reward from "criminal defense" work. The hired gun mentality can take over. Economic reward can become the sole reward for the lawyer, and sooner or later, the lawyer realizes that economic reward is never an end in itself. It seldom motivates or is sufficient to the lawyer in the long term.

The lawyer can be affected in another way. The lawyer may in turn start giving the client limited options with limited information. The lawyer may become a "Yes man," because even where he's wrong, the lawyer wins by increasing control. Or the lawyer becomes unreasonably risk adverse in order to show how much he's protecting the client. In these ways the lawyer can take the delegation of authority and use it to his or her own economic advantage.

These unintended long term effects on the lawyer and client have to be watched carefully and continually monitored. It may be why there is substantial dissatisfaction among lawyers in what it is that they do. It may also be why the Model Rules require the lawyer to keep the client reasonably informed about the means and objectives of the lawsuit.

These are not hypothetical matters. Federal Judge Ann Williams reports her repeated experience with parties who have stopped listening to their lawyers. The attitude she sees from the corporate party, too often, is a "not on my watch" attitude. In others words, "I pay you lawyers a lot of money to make sure that I don't look bad. Make the litigation go away so I won't get in trouble with the board." Judge Williams says she was then often forced to play the role of the legal advisor as the one who says, "You have real exposure here, and you need to go to your board and tell them so." Somehow the client hasn't been able to hear this advice from his lawyer, either because the lawyer has been unwilling to be the bearer of bad news, or because the management simply does not see their lawyer as being an unbiased advice giver.

If the lawyer becomes too much of a lone ranger, the lawyer may not have a sufficient enough relationship with the client to be heard when independent advise needs to be given.

4.8 Lawyer as Friend. Lawyer as Listener

A third model that can structure the lawyer-client relationship is lawyer as friend. This section first describes some of its underlying assumptions to this model. Second, it looks at what techniques the lawyer might use in counseling the client. Finally, it describes some of its uses, benefits, and risks of this model.

4.8.1 **Some Underlying Assumptions**

Many have argued that the previous two models for the lawyer-client relationship are inadequate, and unduly constrain the relationship.[5] The criticisms are basically three-fold:

1. the earlier models assume that the client is unable to make decisions by himself because neither lawyer nor client can truly understand each other's motives;

2. the earlier models overly distrust the opposing party; and

3. the earlier models underestimate the client's altruistic motives.

But how does thinking of yourself as your client's friend, rather than his lawyer and agent problem solver, help to resolve some of these difficulties? To answer that question takes some imagination, and some new assumptions. Let's see where they might lead

First, imagine yourself in need of a listener, not a problem solver. Imagine that you have a moral or ethical dilemma, and you want someone to be your mirror or sounding board for you to clarify your own thinking about a particular problem. Imagine that there are no laws that constrain your behavior. Imagine instead that you could make out your own solutions to your dilemma, once you had thought comprehensively about it, and informed yourself fully about the matter.

1. Getting/Listening. Psychiatrist Tom Rusk contends that the skill of listening is essential to ethical counseling.[6] The issue is whether listening can be taught.

The first thing to do is persuade the lawyer that listening is of vital importance to reaching an understanding of the client's situation, and that reaching an understanding of another's point of

---

5. Much of what follows comes from ideas and discussion that came out of a NITA program called, *Reinventing the Lawyer/Client Relationship*. The intellectual leaders of that group included Maude Pevere and Janeen Kerper. Maude first discussed with us the four-step counseling model, "Get, Give, Merger, Go." She and Janeen also first described to me Tom Rusk's book, *The Power of Ethical Persuasion*, which informs much of my thinking. Again these ideas are more than "just ideas" but have been tested, taught, and used by lawyers in a variety of settings and situations.

6. Tom Rusk, *The Power of Ethical Persuasion* (NY: Viking 1993).

view is crucial to friendship. There are a number of reasons why listening is important. First, it may be your most important tool for showing your intelligence. A leadership project at Stanford indicates that study participants correlated most highly a leader's ability to listen with their intelligence.[7] This makes sense, in a narcissistic way—that we would believe someone else was intelligent who listened to what we had to say and considered it valuable. Think how flattered you are when a teacher remembers, in class, something you said or wrote. Similarly, your ability to demonstrate that you have listened carefully to what the client said implies that you have some wise characteristics: You gather information before you rush to judgment, think comprehensively before you risk expressing an opinion, and manage your own emotional reactions and focus carefully on the task at hand. In other words, you exhibit wisdom.

In addition, listening serves a client relationship purpose. It allows for catharsis. It respects the problem-solving abilities of the speaker. It shares the responsibility for the problem with the one who owns it.

It is important to analyze what gets in the way of listening. Our tendency is to blame the speaker or teacher for our failure. At times, the responsibility does reside with the client speaker, but major problems also lie with the listener. They can be summarized as "self-consciousness." Most important is the fear of failure. We are afraid we will not be able to help, or that our incompetence will be discovered. Additionally, we deal with personal distractions, conflicts of interest and value conflicts, perceived irrelevancies, case threat, ego threat, etiquette barriers, and role expectations.

One way to deal with these distractions is for the lawyer to reorient him or herself about who owns the problem, at the counseling/interviewing stage. Consider how differently you would feel if the client simply said, "Look, what I want is for you to just listen. I don't want your advice. I don't want you to solve my problem for me. All I want is for you to act as my mirror. Help me hear back what I think, and how I feel about my situation. You can do this best by simply listening to what I have to say."

---

7. Id.

Of course, many clients do not want this, in the end. But many do, and most do in the initial stages of their relationship with you. Clients are often unsure about what they should do, and that comes from their lack of knowledge about the legal system, and from their lack of knowledge about themselves as part of the legal problem with which they are dealing.

Consider your own vulnerability when you go to make a major purchase; for example a home or a car. What do you want? What do you need? What is the difference between these two? What role does your view of yourself and all its complexity play in your answer to these questions? If the decision is truly yours to make, think what little help you need from the real estate agent, the car salesman, or even the doctor, at least in that part of the decision which involves what to do.

If the problem-solving role is removed, what listening characteristics start to surface? First, the listener can better quiet fears of inadequacy. After all, the problem is not his to solve. The listener need attend only to whether the speaker is clear, consistent, specific, or conflicted, and attend to how he is feeling about the matter. It is often within the emotional responses that information which the client will need most help in sorting out is found.

Think of the range of emotions clients might have concerning their various legal problems. How might their different emotional states affect the direction they might take in resolving their particular problems? The following chart is taken from Madelyn Burly-Allen's work, *Listening, The Forgotten Skill,* 2d Ed. p.131 (1995).[8]

Here, we encounter **Advanced empathy**. In order to hear, see, and feel these emotions in others, lawyers need to be skilled in:

Quieting the self

Being attentive

Listening with ears, eyes, and insides

Clarifying

---

8. Madelyn Burley-Allen, *Listening, The Forgotten Skill,* 2d Ed. p.131 (1995).

	ANGER	ELATION	DEPRESSION	FEAR
MILD	annoyed	glad	unsure	uneasy
	bothered	pleased	confused	tense
	bugged	amused	bored	concerned
	peeved	contented	resigned	anxious
	irritated	comfortable	disappointed	apprehensive
		surprised	discontented	worried
		relieved	apathetic	
		confident	hurt	
MODERATE	disgusted	cheerful	discouraged	alarmed
	harassed	delighted	drained	shook
	resentful	happy	distressed	threatened
	mad	up	down	afraid
	put upon	elated	unhappy	scared
	set up	great	burdened	frightened
		hopeful	sad	
		eager		
		anticipating		
INTENSE	angry	joyful	miserable	panicky
	contemptuous	excited	ashamed	overwhelmed
	hostile	enthusiastic	crushed	petrified
	hot	turned on	humiliated	terrified
	burned	moved	hopeless	terror-stricken
	furious	enthralled	despairing	
		free	anguished	
		proud		
		fulfilled		
		fascinated		
		titillated		
		engrossing		
		absorbing		

Restating

Reflecting

Summarizing

Validating

Encouraging

They need to resist the temptation to take over, and problem solve by:

Turning off the filters

Not agreeing

Not advising

Not arguing

Not correcting

Not questioning

What does this mean during a counseling session? The psychiatrist, Dr. Tom Rusk argues that the ability to listen is the key to reaching an ethical understanding with another person.[9] Friends seek ethical understanding from each other. Rusk suggests that you confine yourself strictly to the following tasks:

1. Establish that your immediate goal is mutual understanding, not problem solving.

2. Elicit the other person's thoughts, feelings, and desires about the subject at hand.

3. Ask for the other person's help in understanding him or her. Try not to defend or disagree.

4. Repeat the other person's position in your own words to show you understand.

---

9. Tom Rusk, *The Power of Ethical Persuasion* (NY: Viking 1993).

5. Ask the other person to correct your understanding, and keep restating his position.

6. Refer back to your position only to keep things going.

7. Repeat steps 1–6 until the other person unreservedly agrees that you understand his or her position.

2. Give. The next part of the friendship model is for the friend to care enough to give his or her perspective on the problem. This model is different from the standard objective presentation of alternatives and consequences. It requires instead subjective input on the part of the lawyer. It requires that the lawyer "care" whether the client reaches the "right" decision for the client.

What exactly is the "care perspective" and what are its benefits? Care perspective is a moral orientation and a mode of moral thinking that stands in contrast to the justice orientation. The language of the care perspective is still evolving and is admittedly fuzzy. A succinct description comes from A.L. Carse, who says,

> [T]he justice orientation construes the moral point of view as (1) an impartial point of view, (2) which understands particular moral judgments as derived from abstract and universal principles, (3) which sees moral judgment as essentially dispassionate rather than passionate, and (4) it emphasizes individual rights and norms of formal equality and reciprocity in modeling our moral relationships.

> By contrast, the care orientation (1) rejects impartiality as an essential mark of the moral, (2) understands moral judgments as situation-attuned perceptions sensitive to others' needs and to the dynamics of particular relationships, (3) construes moral reasoning as involving empathy and concern, and (4) emphasizes norms of responsiveness and responsibility in our relationships with others.

What would a decision-making process that is modeled on care look like, and how would such a process resist the constraints that arise from the role playing hierarchical model? An individual approaching the previous case from the care perspective would proceed as follows.

First, the provider would identify the persons involved in interdependent relationships in this situation. For the legal practitioner, it violates an exclusive focus on the client. The opinions of all persons in significant relationships with the one cared for are considered. The lawyer's opinion is also included, because he's also in a significant relationship by virtue of his involvement with the client.

The second step of the friend/decision-making process is the most radical. It identifies the central issue of care, and addresses what caring demands in this particular situation, with these particular persons, to strengthen (or at least maintain) their primary relationships and avoid hurt and harm. This step can only be taken after identifying the interdependent parties and their primary relationships. One then considers the view of both the client and those in the other relationships: customers, employees, suppliers, shareholders, family, or friends.

These steps provide for the subjectivity that friendship requires. It allows for moral self-expression. It necessitates a true understanding of, and reflection upon, the feelings of others, yet doesn't designate to one individual or another, the moral responsibility for the decision. The role taken by the lawyer is more of a facilitator of the discussion, or consensus builder, than problem solver.

3. Merge. Third, a friend should discuss and think through all possible alternative activities to determine which are "loving and just" to those who are involved. He should ask how the action will affect each person's life, including their shared life. The perspective of the friend arises from this attempt to enter into and understand the context of the situation. The friend enters the situation and participates as one caring, whose view is to be communicated to the parties involved and carefully considered. Again, any actions proposed, and the consequences of proposed alternatives, are evaluated in terms of whether they are "loving and just" for the individuals and their shared life.[10]

A friend and counselor does not necessarily go along with the client's decision. In this model, the friend takes moral responsibility for whether he joins the client's decision. If he cannot, then he withdraws from the partnership. The friendship model protects the lawyer from necessarily joining in every client's ventures. It allows for the moral self to discuss, and disagree, on courses of action.

4. Go. Finally, assuming a successful merger has been reached, the involved parties jointly should select an acceptable alternative, anticipate objections and answer them, and devise a workable

---

10. Again, lawyers can learn from psychiatry. Rusk has three steps to creating resolutions. They are:

1. Affirm your mutual understanding and confirm that you are both ready to consider options for resolution.

2. Brainstorm multiple options.

3. If a mutually agreeable solution is not obvious, try one or more of the following:

    a. Take time out to reconsider, consult, exchange proposals and reconvene.

    b. Agree to neutral arbitration, mediation, or counseling.

    c. Compromise between alternative solutions.

    d. Take turns between alternative solutions.

    e. Yield (for now) once your position is thoroughly and respectfully considered.

    f. Assert your positional power after thoroughly and respectfully considering their position.

    g. Agree to disagree and still respect each other; then, if you can, go your separate ways on the particular issue. Rusk, *The Power of Ethical Persuasion*, at 148.

plan for carrying out the proposed solution.[11] After the decision is carried out, it is also helpful to evaluate its adequacy. The friendship model assumes that this "Listen, Give, Merge, Go" model will create more meaningful lawyer-client relationships, which will better represent the holistic client and build more shared decision making. The aim is that both the practice of law and client satisfaction will be more enhanced.

4.9 Choosing The Right Model for The Right Client/Situation

It is important to recognize that, beyond their practical limitations, surrogate and friendship models have Code of Professional Responsibility limitations. The Model Rules of Responsibility, Rule 1.2, prohibit the extreme power structure of a "hired gun surrogate" model by requiring that a lawyer "consult with the client as to the means by which [client objectives] are to be pursued." Rule 1.4 also states that a lawyer:

> (a) shall keep a client reasonably informed about the status of a matter . . . and (b) shall explain a matter to the extent reasonably necessary to permit the client to make informed decisions regarding the representation."

Of course, if the client does not want to know, who is to complain? But if the client changes his or her mind, then the Model Rules become a sword against the lawyer, a risk of which the surrogate lawyer should be particularly wary.

Regarding the friendship model, the lawyer's concern about gathering salient facts and getting input from various other parties in relationships with the client should not overstep client confidentiality requirements. Model Rule 1.6 obligates the lawyer to protect the confidences of the client. Comment 1 to Model Rule 1.3 also limits the friendship model:

---

11. As a possible final step, the counselor might consider drafting an agreement which can memorialize the agreed-upon solutions. Such a process suggests bargaining over the rights and duties of the parties. At least one commentator feels that bargaining is not a useful tool, and is antithetical to a care perspective. See, Annette Baier, *Trust and Antitrust*, 96 Ethics 231, (1986)(hereinafter Baier) (Baier criticizes contractarians because they ignore the costs to relationships from adversarial self-interested bargaining.)

> A lawyer should pursue a matter on behalf of a client despite opposition, obstruction or personal inconvenience to the lawyer, and may take whatever lawful and ethical measures are required to vindicate a client's cause or endeavor. A lawyer should act with commitment and dedication to the interests of the client and with zeal in advocacy upon the client's behalf.

In other words, the merge must not produce lukewarm, half-hearted representation, nor be a heavy-handed attempt by the lawyer to impose his morality on the client.

Having said this, the friendship model can be an attractive alternative for some clients. The new or burgeoning business client is a prime example. Many of these clients have long been interested in having more from their lawyer than just technical legal advice. They want them to be a partner; to care whether the business succeeds in the long term; to understand what is really important to the client, which is often more than short term, bottom line profits.

A subset of the business lawyer setting, where friendship seems to be in vogue, is the "in-house" counsel, or the lawyer who heads a corporate acquisition team. These lawyers must not only be able to advocate the client's interests, but understand them well enough to move in a strong way when the interests of the client demand creative, responsive action. The friend analogy, where deep trust has been built on the basis of understanding and moral discussion, explains why the lawyer can act so forcefully and accurately for the client.

Interestingly enough, the same is true of a good domestic relations lawyer. Some clients want, first and foremost, a trusting relationship. They want someone who understands not only what they think, but how they feel. They need both emotional support and tough love. They need to be "bucked up" when they are momentarily depressed, and brought into touch with reality when they are feeling unrealistically powerful and in control. In other words, they would rather have a friend who made the occasional mistake, than the dispassionate, disinterested analysis of a hired gun.

In summary, the "friendship model" should be explored in a number of areas. First, the lawyer should consider the "friendship model" wherever the lawyer is asked to deal with individuals who are, or will be, in long-term relationships with each other. In the commercial arena, for example, lawyers may be asked to be lawyers for "the deal," in the drafting of corporate documents for small closely held corporations, or in drafting partnership agreements that could affect the parties for years to come. These situations always seem to put the lawyer in an impossible situation. They continually need to trade short-term risk and gain for long-term gain, and building relationships of trust. The ethic of care, and the friendship model, can structure the lawyer's role, and provide guidance about what to do and say. Similarly, the lawyer should consider the "friendship model" where he acts as trustee for trusts with multiple beneficiaries. Family legal problems, problems with the placement and care of children, situations involving bioethical issues, and those involving the elderly also seem to be potentially useful.

On the other hand, the friendship model is probably not useful for problems between strangers, where the concept of the web of relatedness doesn't seem to fit. For example, questions of torts, products liability, and crimes between strangers seem less promising. When impartial issues of justice and fairness are the heart of the conflict, the rights-based model may be more appropriate and thus preferable. But where the situation involves individuals in strong relationships with each other, it only makes sense that early involvement of these others is crucial, both to gathering accurate information and understanding what care demands of the people involved. It requires the lawyer to break the bounds of rights analysis, and seek particularized, human solutions that better fit the people involved.

4.10 Client-Centered Counseling and The Institutional Client

How does one counsel the corporate, government, or institutional client? Client-centered autonomy based model that gives weight to an individual's social, psychology, and moral values seem out of place. How does a lawyer befriend an organization? So delegation based on fiduciary relationship seems to be in order. Still the assignment comes from individual officers and managers.

What will protect the institution from either the unconscious biases of either the lawyer or the institution officer or spokesperson?

In these situations, while an officer or manager may speak for the institution, the client is bigger and more diverse in its interests and risk preferences than the one officer who is speaking for the client. In these situations, it is not the officer's feelings, risk preferences or morality that ultimately governs the situations outcomes. Is the lawyer free to impose his own economic preferences and moral code on forming the legal strategy? What is a client-centered counselor to do where the client has "no butt to kick, and no soul to damn?"

Expert litigation consultants have developed a set of decision making principles or factors to help guide them in building a consensus where there may be a division in interests between the officer, the lawyer, and the institution.

Medical professionals and institutions are in analogous situation with patients. Just as a surgeon may prefer to cut on a patient, and hospital to recommend extended hospital visits, the Hippocratic oath is all that protects the patient from the doctor's preferences and biases. The field of bioethics has been created to develop bioethical principles to guide doctors, hospitals and patients in their decisions. Similarly, lawyers need to create a set of principles or factors to help guide the client in forming the appropriate strategy or treatment plan. This approach borrows its structure and framework from moral philosophy.

On a meta-ethical level, ethical systems can be classified as teleological (or rule based systems) or utilitarian (or principled based systems). In their extreme, rule based decisions are critiqued for their lack of flexibility and individualization, and principled based systems based on abstract obligations to do good and do no harm are criticized for there inconsistent and self serving applications. One way to integrate the two is to develop a rule utilitarian model, or one that sets up rules in the service of the greater good. Such a principled based system seems to be most useful for professional counseling where autonomy is de-emphasized either because the client is in crisis, or where the client is an institution. In these situation expert experience is particularly useful, and can draw on experience and insights to develop rules or principles that can best serve the institutional client. Using these rules, reference points or principles to guide the decision, keeps the decision from being hijacked to the benefit of one of the particular players in the decision-making process.

One set of rules that operate nicely along side the litigation process for the institutional client are as follows:

Peace first

Lowest cost to execute

Simplest to execute

Least public exposure

Deanne Siemer of the Wilse Group, Washington D.C., (an expert at advising institutions with major litigation problems) describes the principles this way,

Peace first	Many clients like their lawyers to be warriors, but "peace" options should always be considered thoroughly before any "war" options are used. This comes under the general principle of "Don't make the problem worse."
Lowest cost	The lowest-cost option deserves the hardest look. The cost of legal matters tends to escalate and cost estimates tend to be optimistic. Most clients would rather spend the marginal dollar on their business or personal matters rather than legal contests.
Simplest to execute	Execution of legal strategies is always risky because few clients have extensive experience in managing legal matters, so they are likely to be difficult for the lawyer to control. The option that is simplest to execute is often the least risky.
Least public exposure	Most companies and individuals operate largely out of the glare of public opinion and, for that reason, they tend to ignore or underestimate the costs of publicity and adverse public opinion in legal matters. Avoiding public exposure where possible avoids a risk that may have unknown proportions.

These rules are important to winnow down the options that the spokesperson or officer of institution should be considering. It assumes that they will put the institutions interests above their own and it keeps the immediate decision maker on track to head in a satisfactory out come for the institution.

How might these principles shape the counseling session with an institutional client' representative. Deanne Siemer takes the rules she uses in guiding her decisions with clients and makes them the foundation of a counseling chart. Combining these rules with a mathematical weighing system she gives some suggestions that make for a detailed and wise analysis for forming a legal strategy with an institutional client.

Siemer uses the *Homestead* problem, Part I, as an example:

> When applying the general rules for comparative purposes, using a numerical rating rather than descriptive words usually yields a better result. What one person means by "low" may be quite different from what another person means by the same word. However if a scale of 1 to 5 is applied, with 1 as the lowest score and 5 as the highest, the total score usually is a good reflection of the comparison.

A matrix listing the options on the vertical axis and the general rules on the horizontal axis will permit ready comparisons. Use numerical ratings ranging from 1 to 5 or 1 to 10, depending on how many options you have. If there are relatively few options, a 1 to 5 scale should suffice. In this case, we have twelve potential options, so a scale of 1 to 10 might be better.

Each option is ranked relative to each other option with respect to one of the general rules. Using scores in a matrix is not to suggest that there is a "right" total score; only that a rough scoring can weed out some options as compared to others. The purpose of the matrix is to answer the question: "Compared to what?" So, for example, with respect to the general rule favoring "least adverse public exposure," the question is which of the options is *most* likely to generate adverse public exposure. Litigation is a very public option, so one might give it a low score in this regard. Then the question is what option is the *least* likely to get public attention. The informal mediation and informal persuasion options tend to be very private if handled properly. They might seem less likely to draw adverse attention than the other options. Then other options are compared to the best and worst and among themselves. The question is whether this option is more, less, or equally likely to generate adverse public exposure than some other option.

Here is an example of a matrix. A rating of 1 indicates no compliance with the general rule. A rating of 5 indicates very good compliance with the general rule. Higher total scores indicate better options.

⬇ ➡	Peace first	Low cost	Simple execution	Least public exposure	Total score
Sue	1	1	1	1	4
Demand letter	1	8	8	3	20
Sell	3	2	1	2	8
Convert to condos, sell	3	1	1	2	7
Spin off	3	5	5	4	17
Joint projects with A-Best	6	3	1	3	13
Go negative	1	4	4	1	10
Go positive	8	4	4	2	18
Change management	6	5	5	4	20
Informal mediation	9	6	7	8	30
Informal persuasion	9	9	8	9	35
Do nothing	10	10	10	8	38

One can (and should) argue in your team about the relative scores. This is a way to examine assumptions, compare ideas, and stimulate creative thinking about the problem. In simplified form, using part I of the *Homestead* case, (Homestead worries that A-Best Homes is engaged in product disparagement of their homes, saying that they are termite infested,) the discussion might be something like the outline below.

Sue	Litigation is not a peaceful solution; it is not a low cost solution; it is rarely simple to execute because the client has control of only its part of the process; there is a great deal of potential public exposure, particularly where electronic filing is used because all records are not only publicly available but completely searchable.
Demand letter	A demand letter asks that the derogatory statements be stopped and threatens to sue if they are not. A demand letter points to litigation, so it is not a very peaceful solution although the letter itself does not initiate any litigation. A demand letter itself is relatively low cost, usually only the time of the lawyer to write it and the time of the client to approve it. However, a demand letter may require additional research into the law or facts, and often leads to a reply and further replies, thus multiplying the cost. It is simple in initial execution; most lawyers have form letters for this sort of thing. However, the follow-up may not be so simple. A demand letter holds some potential for public exposure as it may be delivered by the recipient to others.
Sell	The option of selling the business is probably a relatively peaceful solution, but it may entail considerable expenses and is not simple to execute. There is some risk of adverse public exposure because of due diligence on the part of the buyer.
Convert to condos and sell	This is like the option of selling the entire business but more complicated. The cost may be higher in the short run; and the public exposure is likely to be greater because of the risks involved in dealing with individual apartment dwellers.
Spin off	This option establishes a new identity for the Florida-Georgia apartment rental part of the business, but does not remove the problems from Homestead which would remain the owner of the separate business entity created in the spin-off process. A spin off is less complicated and costly than other corporate options, but it can attract public attention as it appears to be a corporate maneuver and encourages speculation as to its "real" purpose.

Joint projects with A-Best	This has the prospect of being a peaceful solution and could be the best possible outcome depending on the terms and commercial viability, all of which are unknown. The cost of devising and negotiating a joint project might be considerable because this is quite a complicated solution, probably at least as complicated and perhaps more complicated than selling.
Go negative	Negative advertising criticizing A-Best is not a peaceful solution, and it generates a very public controversy. It entails cash outlays for the advertising content and media placement, and has some difficulty of executing well.
Go positive	Positive advertising extolling the virtues of Homestead's housing is a fairly peaceful solution. It has about the same cost and difficulty of execution as the negative advertising would, and it could generate counter advertising by A-Best which could create adverse public exposure.
Change management	Changing the management company to improve conditions at the apartment complexes and thereby reduce adverse comment is a peaceful solution as far as A-Best is concerned, but could create some difficulty with the management company that is being fired. It may be a low cost option that is simple to execute if there are competing management companies available to take on the assignment and the contract with the existing management company allows Homestead the flexibility to change.
Informal mediation	Informal mediation is a peaceful option if the mediator is skilled and experienced. It is relatively low cost, although good mediators can have fairly high hourly rates. In some cases informal mediators do not charge for their services. For example, a trade association may help mediate disputes among members. A mediation might take only half a day, in which case the mediator's fee may not be a significant expense. Mediation is normally entirely confidential and has almost no risk of public exposure.
Informal persuasion	Informal persuasion is usually a peaceful option if handled skillfully. It is a relatively low cost option, particularly if someone from the company is the person selected to carry out this task. Making an overture to persuade is usually simple to execute and carries little risk of adverse public exposure.
Do nothing	Doing nothing is a peaceful option. It is a low cost option because the lawyer and client are basically waiting to see if anything further happens. Whatever damage has been done by the prior statements may entail costs, but if no further statements are made, there is no additional cost incurred from this option. It is simple to execute, and has low public exposure.

This comparative analysis suggests that suing A-Best, based on what we now know, is a "worst" option and should be the first to be discarded because there are other viable options. This is almost always the case. Litigation is expensive and risky. It may be the end game of the strategy if the client absolutely must reach an objective that ultimately can be had only by successful litigation. That is most likely not the case here. Homestead can operate its rental units in the face of A-Best's criticisms, although that might be more difficult and expensive than if A-Best stopped its derogatory statements.

The option of "going negative" might be discarded at this stage as well, as it has significant downside risks (war-like option and considerable public exposure).

The transaction oriented options also seem relatively less desirable because they probably involve significant cost and would be more difficult to execute than some other available options.

The matrix exercise has allowed the strategist to discard four or five of the options.

In the words of that great sage and songwriter Kenny Rogers:

> *Every gambler knows*
> *The secret to surviving*
> *Is knowing what to throw away*
> *And knowing what to keep*
>
> 'Cause every hand's a winner
> And every hand's a loser . . . [12]

4.10.1 Focus on The Risk of Being Wrong To Select The Best Options

There may be no one "right" answer as to the strategy to be followed; however there is almost always a right answer about the relative amount of risk that is involved with a particular strategy option compared to other available options.

---

12. "The Gambler." Song written by Don Schlitz; popularized by singer Kenny Rogers.

Most inexperienced lawyers are too optimistic in making judgments about risk in a legal strategy situation. For that reason, it is a good idea for the lawyer to (1) think about the downside; and (2) express opinions in terms of numbers, not words like "good," or "pretty good," or "likely." Using numbers ensures that the participants in the development of the strategy all understand each other.

Here	With respect to the current situation, how much risk is there that we are wrong on the facts. There are certain facts that are key to a particular option being the right route to the desired outcome. What is the relative risk that we are wrong in what we now know?
There	In this case, assume the client's objective is simply having A-Best make no more adverse statements. With respect to the desired outcome, how much risk is there of not getting to that outcome in following a particular option?
Time	How long is the option likely to take? Is this option within the client's available time? In a situation such as this one, where the time constraint may be flexible, ask what is the relative position of each option with respect to the time it might take to get to a resolution.
Resources	What is the option likely to cost? Is this option within the client's available money? What is the relative risk with respect to the amount of investment that will be required by the client to carry out this option? This factor includes the amount of legal research potentially needed to ensure that an option is either available or executed correctly.

Create another matrix and write out a comparison of the remaining options. This matrix assesses fewer options, so its ratings could be on a simpler 1 to 5 scale. You may not get the numbers right in the absolute sense, but you probably will get the relationships among the options right. This is also a good vehicle for lawyers working as a team to pool their views. And it provides a good outline for explaining a strategy to the client. (The matrix itself is not often used with the client, but having worked through the matrix, the lawyer's explanation is usually more organized.)

Here is a sample risk matrix. A rating of 1 means relatively little risk; a rating of 5 means quite a lot of risk. Low total scores indicate better options. Note that this risk matrix works in the opposite way (low score means better option) than the general rules matrix (high score means better option). The reversal of the scoring helps stimulate careful thought.

⬇️➡️	HERE	THERE	TIME	MONEY	TOTAL
	Risk that key facts are wrong	Risk that outcome is not reached	Risk as to amount of time	Risk as to investment required	Risk
Informal persuasion (20)	1	2	1	1	5
Do nothing (19)	1	4	1	1	7
Mediate informally (17)	2	3	1	2	8
Change management (15)	3	4	4	4	15
Spin off (14)	3	5	4	5	17
Demand letter (13)	4	5	3	3	15
Go positive (12)	4	4	2	3	13

Informal persuasion	The risks with respect to informal persuasion seem relatively low. While there is some risk that this option will not be effective in getting A-Best to stop making derogatory statements, that risk seems lower than most of the other options. A skillful effort at persuasion probably presents less risk than doing nothing, and probably presents less risk than mediation in which the two sides confront each other in a framework designed for disputes. The time and money risks are lower than other options. Informal persuasion would not necessarily involve legal time.
Do nothing	There is no commitment to any particular facts in the "do nothing" option, so there is relatively little risk with respect to the facts being wrong. There may be a higher risk of a bad outcome, however, if a totally passive option is selected. No time or money will be expended in this option (except to monitor the situation), so there is basically no risk of being wrong as to those factors.
Mediate informally	In mediation, there is more commitment to a particular version of the facts, and therefore more exposure if the facts are wrong. Informal mediation is a low risk option with respect to a bad outcome because a skilled neutral party tries to help achieve a workable outcome for both parties. The time and costs of mediation are usually well-defined because the process is short and participants are limited.
Change management	Management may have nothing to do with the underlying causes of the derogatory statements, so the option to change management presents a relatively high risk of not achieving the desired outcome. On the other hand, new management might mitigate the damage from any derogatory statements by active work at good relations with tenants. The relative risk of being wrong about the time and expense of changing management may be considerable, particularly if Homestead has never done this before.
Spin off	A spin off would separate the Florida/Georgia business from the rest of the company, but may be too late to insulate Homestead (the main company) from the risk of tenant litigation or regulatory fines. Therefore, compared to the other options, the risks of not achieving the desired outcome, and spending more time and money than anticipated, appear greater. Some additional legal research might be needed to support a spin off option, depending on the firm's experience in this area.

Demand letter	A demand letter might provoke A-Best to retaliate, which would mean that the desired outcome might be farther from Homestead's reach than under other options. A demand letter requires Homestead to take a firm position on the facts (and, by implication, also the law) which involves more exposure to the risk of being wrong on the facts. A demand letter looks to litigation as the end game, and litigation seems impractical here.
Go positive	Positive advertising has some risk of being wrong on the facts. If Homestead advertises "resistant to hurricane-force winds" for example and that is not true, the company could have multiplied its problems by creating false advertising. Positive advertising also does not get at the root of the problem directly, if A-Best is making derogatory statements; it attempts to mitigate the damage from those statements.

Positive advertising has some risk of being wrong on the facts. If Homestead advertises "resistant to hurricane-force winds" for example and that is not true, the company could have multiplied its problems by creating false advertising. Positive advertising also does not get at the root of the problem directly, if A-Best is making derogatory statements; it attempts to mitigate the damage from those statements.

It is important to emphasize that there is no magic in any particular rating. The effort is to assess relative risk when picking among viable options. The matrix provides a vehicle for asking, "Is this option more risky than these other options with respect to this single factor?" A low number is *less* risk.

For example, with respect to the risk that the time estimate is too short, the options of changing management and spinning off the apartment complex business present the most unknowns at present, and thus the most risk as to that particular factor. The demand letter may create a long chain of accusatory correspondence and generating the positive advertising may take longer than now anticipated, so the time risk, while less than spin off or changing management, could be significant.

In this case, the strategist might conclude that while the spin off, demand letter and positive advertising options are viable, they have higher relative risk than other options. For that reason, the strategist might look first to the remaining options in fashioning a strategy.

4.10.2 Assemble The Best Options into A Process

Strategy is a process. The process identifies a starting point and, if the actions proposed as the starting point do not achieve the defined objective, then the process continues with a second move, and so on. For this reason, the strategy may incorporate a number of the available options.

The features of this principled approach to forming legal strategy are obvious. It has integrated many features of the client-centered, delegation, and friendship model into a practical set of factors that can frame the choice to institutions client representative. It provides information about the economic, social, and psychological consequences of decisions and assumes the institution will favor a risk adverse, cost effective, simple and humble solution. It also balances out the litigator's tendency and preference to want to go to war.

4.11 Conclusion

In the end, the rule utilitarian model maybe best for all kinds of client, individual, corporate, non profit, or institutional. After all rules, peace first, low cost, simple solution, low profile, capture the long term interests of most of us. Still, there is a need to consider justice concerns. Perhaps the client wants justice. Perhaps there is too much at stake for the client to take anything less than a win. Perhaps there is a need to establish precedent. Perhaps they want to win as a matter of principle. These kinds of disputes may require a different set of factors and or hierarchy of analysis.

And maybe it is where we these justice concerns raise their heads that the learn can start to discern when litigation is the best option. The next chapter explores the legal strategy of negotiation and mediated solutions.

❮·❯ ❮·❯ ❮·❯

FURTHER READING

Books

Tom Rusk, *The Power of Ethical Persuasion*, (NY: Viking 1993).

David A. Binder, Paul Bergman, and Susan C. Price, *Lawyer as Counselor: A Client-Centered Approach* (West Publishing, 1991, 2004).

Articles

Articles in George M. Cohen and Susan P. Koniak, *Foundations of the Law and Ethics of Lawyering* (2004).

Paul J. Zwier, *The Ethics of Care and Re-Imagining the Lawyer Client Relationship,* 22 J. CONTEMP. LAW 383 (1996).

CHAPTER FIVE

TESTING A STRATEGY THROUGH NEGOTIATION
AND MEDIATION

*It is difficult to distinguish deduction from what in other circumstances
is called problem-solving. . . .*
> —Frank Smith (b. 1928), Canadian educator. *To Think*, ch. 2,
> Teachers College Press (1990).

*The quality of decision is like the well-timed swoop of a falcon
which enables it to strike and destroy its victim.*
> —Sun Tzu (6–5th century B.C.), Chinese general. *The Art
> of War*, ch. 5, axiom 13 (c. 490 B.C.), ed. by James Clavell
> (1981).

Strategic planning requires the lawyer to think strategically regarding furthering the client's goals and implementing the client's
objectives. It requires that the lawyer not only understand the "end
game" if other dispute resolution processes fail, but it means the
lawyer must understand different dispute resolution methods and
the strengths and weaknesses of each.

For example, lawyers must understand not only negotiation
strategy, the ins and outs of mediation, and the pitfalls of arbitration, but also bankruptcy law, intellectual property law, antitrust
law, and the companion procedural laws regarding removal, join-
der, interpleader, multi-district litigation, and class actions. Regardless of the process and substantive law setting in which the lawyer
works, the lawyer must always see the process as a means to the
client's objectives, and be willing to consider switching, when possible, from one process and setting to another if another process
might work better to serve the client's goals.

At the heart of each of these frameworks for dispute resolution
lays negotiation theory and practice and the complementary field
of conflict resolution. They are keys to a lawyer's understanding
the strategies involved of different dispute resolution processes
and settings. This chapter will focus on negotiation and conflict

resolution theory, as it informs lawyer strategy in every step of the litigation process, but in particular, as it informs how the lawyer should best implement the client's objectives.

5.1 **Preliminary Perspectives**

A vital part of dispute resolution is the management of information; what you give to the other parties and what you get from the other side. Information is the key to the accurate evaluation of the dispute, and a vital element in the prediction of the likely outcome.[1] Understanding how information management affects outcomes will help the litigator strategically plan for conflict resolution that will best serve the client's goals.

In some ways then, the litigation process itself, (whether finally resolved by the parties, or with the help of a mediator or adjudicator) is one big negotiation and information exchange process. The litigation process is the default, and is itself designed so that the parties learn about each other's facts, values, perspectives on law, predictions of outcome, and, if the parties do not resolve their dispute for themselves, the court learns about these same facts, values, perspectives on law, and predictions of outcomes, and reaches a decision. In litigation, each side discovers as best it can the others view of the predicted value of the case in the eyes of the decision maker and if there is any overlap, the parties settle. It is a decision-making process that is based on economics, rationality, and wealth maximization.

Settlement is the outcome in 99 percent of civil cases so the process seems to work well most times in the non-criminal context. Where liberty interests are at stake it is another matter. Some times parties complain about the expense of getting themselves in a position to determine the value of the case. Still, under the position bargaining model of negotiation, the process is designed to empower the parties to settle when they rationally should settle. Even where the parties resort to a court, the court's decision itself may not finally resolve the dispute, but instead provide the parties with further information and leverage to reach even a different and better settlement that better fits their needs.

---

1. Robert M. Bastress and Joseph D. Harbaugh, *Interviewing, Counseling, and Negotiation: Skills for Effective Representation* 488–522 (1990).

It is important to recognize the values inherent in the adversary system. The traditional approach to litigation is premised on the model that better decisions are made if each side must test its information by evidence in front of an unbiased decision maker. This process is based on the model of a fight, or competitive game, rather than on the basis of a cooperative model bent on getting at the truth.

5.2 **Position Bargaining**

Imbedded in the adversarial process is a position bargaining model of dispute resolution. The parties both seek information that will allow them to value their cases, and hide information from the other side that might give the other side an opportunity to take advantage. From the information they are able to discover each party then determines whether there is any overlap between their positions, and seeks by threats and persuasion to move the other side closer and closer to its bottom line position, the position at which it would rather take a settlement rather than risk the uncertain outcome of a trial.

The parties do not provide information to each other freely.[2] They seek to only inform the other side about those facts that they must turn over because of discovery rules. The adversarial nature of the process is inherent in the rules that dictate what the parties responsibilities are with regard to discovery. Information exchange in negotiation also seems to be driven by the assumption that you have uncertain information, at best, about your opponent's weaknesses, and if you settle out of court before putting people under oath at trial, you risk settling for too much or too little. Position bargaining strategies best test what cards the other side actually holds. Your positions serve as bets in the gamble of litigation, and **may** inform each side on what cards each holds. Position bargainers use their positions to get information, and the willingness to settle, and while often, this combination of factors occurs on the court house steps, it might also occur after jury selection, opening statements, after the jury has started to deliberate, or even on appeal.

---

2. The new Federal Rules of Civil Procedure tries to change this by requiring information exchanges. Still the risk of discovery is that the other side has not revealed everything, and so the court must test its evidence at trial.

A classic example of position bargaining occurs in the bazaar or market place. Imagine you are at an open air market in Beijing. You stop at a table and pick up a shirt. The vendor says, "You like? For you, special price. 100 yuan." You say, "Too much." The vendor says, "How much?" You say, "30 yuan." The vendor says, "No, how about two shirts for 150 yuan." You say, "No, the most I pay is 50 yuan." They say no. You start to walk a way. They say, "Fine," and throw the shirt at you. You pay 50 yuan.

Position bargainers use positions to get information about what the other side really thinks. They posture and bluff to try to force movement. They provide little information about why or how they determine the price. We don't know what the buyer wants the shirt for, or how much the seller has in mark up or carrying costs. Reasons are not given. The parties think of the exchange as purely voluntary. Each may use psychology, and threats, and try to raise the sunk costs of each side by dragging out the time of bargaining. They may use the pressure of the public audience to shame the other into moving. But in the end, the process is governed by getting information by taking positions, to test what each side thinks the transaction is worth.

5.2.1 An Analytical Economic Model

Assume, for a minute, however, that each side had perfect information about the other side's case. Assume that discovery has been completed and each side has all that it can legally expect to get. Position bargainers still must predict the outcome at trial as a way of determining the fair price of resolving the dispute. Every lawyer knows the dangers of prediction. Predicting victory can raise false expectations in the client, making the client spend the money before the client gets it. It also subjects the lawyer to the, "but you said" from the client, when the prediction doesn't come true. Still, the client is entitled to make an informed decision when giving the lawyer settlement authority for negotiation purposes. The question is whether economic models which use probabilities will provide the useful language of prediction in order for the client to make informed decisions. In fact, the question of whether to use probabilities may be moot, because clients seem to be demanding as much. Certainly business clients and client insurers want a probability of success in order to set up reserves, and consumers demand it of their doctors, so why not of their lawyers?

In order to use economics and probabilities to provide the client with information about what his case is worth, the lawyer first needs to be clear about what economic modeling and what probabilities really provide. The beauty of economic analysis is that for every real world problem that makes prediction impossible, you simply make an assumption. And the result is a "mathematic-like" formula that gives the appearance of a scientific method, or certainty, and of objectivity. Perhaps it gives a false impression. In addition, a second dangerous assumption the economist makes is that jurors are rational. The client also assumes perfect information about a case will be produced by the litigation process and trial. The question is whether these assumptions are so false and will so cloud any probabilities so as to make the probabilities misleading rather that helpful.

On the other, the lawyer needs to start some place in communicating his legal assessment of the case, and with these two assumptions in mind, the lawyer can start to calculate how jurors will likely calculate damages in a given case. Analytically A and strategically speaking, we might be able to create a formula that will make us more precise in valuing our case, and enable us to better inform the client about what to expect. The corollary benefits are also substantial. A byproduct of making an economic calculation for cases in order to place a value on the case provides more information to the client so that he can truly control the outcome. A second by-product of using economic tools will be to give the lawyers more persuasive arguments in their negotiations about what the case is worth, and provide the language to move their opponents off of their position, (provided our reasoning doesn't open up counter arguments to our disadvantage.)

As we've said, before actually communicating with the client, the lawyer should look at the case from the perspective of the jury, or the end game. First, in a typical tort situation (assuming the jury has perfect information, as presented through the trial process), the jury will need to determine the percentage of fault of each party. It then adds up the fault attributed to the defendants, (depending on joint and several liability rules) and subtracts the amount of fault attributed to the plaintiff to come up with percentages of liability. Of course, in a jurisdiction that is not a "pure comparative" jurisdiction, this works, but the juries' figuring close cases in "50 percent jurisdictions," (where the plaintiff is barred from recovery where the plaintiff's fault is equal to or greater than the defendant's), may make them lean toward the plaintiff to make sure the plaintiff gets something—at least if they know about the results of finding 49 or 50 percent liability on the part of the plaintiff. Some jurisdictions don't tell the jury.

Second, if the jury determines there is compensable liability, then the jury needs to figure damages. Damages are made up of "hard damages" like:

1. past medicals, in personal injury cases and

2. past lost income figures, (loss of business from product disparagement) and then moves to "softer damages," including

3. predictions on future medical expenses,

4. and future loss income, to "softest damages," for

5. pain and suffering, or

6. humiliation and mental anguish, or

7. loss of consortium, or

8. loss of "hedonic" damages (the pleasure of playing the piano),

9. loss to future trade, and

10. punitive damages, to send a message to the defendant and like defendants to deter future behavior.

Third, the jury will need to multiply the percentage of fault times the total amount of damages found. Or, depending on joint and several liability rules, it simply takes the total damages and subtracts the percentage of fault attributed to the plaintiff to come up with a figure for damages.

Yet in predicting what the jury will actually do in such a case, the lawyer knows that there are "non-rational" factors that the jury may take into account. The particular judge may exercise a lot of subtle control over the process. Marginally relevant good or bad facts[3] may significantly affect the outcome. The jury may consciously or subconsciously take race into account, age, or sex, or may be biased against corporations, or angry at institutions and governments who make their lives difficult, especially where injury occurs to protected classes like elderly, pregnant women, or children, for example. The lawyer on the other side may be a particularly wonderful communicator, having demonstrated talent in bringing in spectacular verdicts for her clients. Finally, the make-up of the jury needs to be considered, as jury verdicts of big city, certain Southern rural counties, and or minority juries tend to give more to some plaintiffs and other rural or suburban juries and upper or middle class jurors may give less. Selecting potential jurors from driver license registration versus voter registration can make a large difference.

To factor these biases into an economic calculation, lawyers may try to determine a **multiplier**—the amount that they multiply, times the "hard" economic damages in the case, to come up with a prediction as to what the jury will do.[4] Certain jurisdictions try to keep tabs on how much juries give in relation to the "hard" damages in the case. Historically, Philadelphia or New York may have a multiplier of 4.5 to 5. Chesterfield, Virginia may have a multiplier of 2 to 3. Of course, any given case can and should be distinguished from the average verdicts (just as with any jury verdict service), arguing even about what are hard damages. Additionally, there are definitional problems with multipliers: for example, should future loss income be counted as hard damages in a particular case, or, should pain and suffering be greater or lesser when death was imminent? Still the multiplier can be a way of predicting how much over the hard damages that the jury might pay in a given jurisdiction.

So, in a given case, a lawyer might value a personal injury case as follows—

---

3. For example, evidence that one of the parties is a saint or that one is not a nice person.

4. These multipliers may be less relevant in commercial litigation where the sympathy factors or the community's views have less effect when the dispute is between two parties that can take care of themselves. Or maybe they still do play a role, especially depending on the good will that company may have built up because of its community involvement and corporate image.

Hospital $30,000

Future hospital (dis)* $60,000

Loss wages (+ int) $50,000

Future lost wages (dis)* $500,000

            Total Specials $640,000

            Multiplier 4.5 = $2,880,000

$30,000 hospital

$60,000 future hospital (dis)*

$50,000 loss wages (+ int)

$500,000 future lost wages (dis)*

            Total Specials $640,000

            Multiplier 4.5 = $2,880,000

The difference is presumably made up in pain and suffering, emotional distress, and the like.

Further, the attorney needs to predict percentage of liability to plaintiff, say 30 percent.

            30 percent of $2,880,000 = $864,000

            Net Damages   **$2,016,000**

Now, assuming that the probability figure is accurate, $2,016,000 is the lawyer's prediction of the most likely jury damages award.

Or take for instance, the *Homestead* case at the preliminary injunction stage. Here the prediction is about what the judge will likely do. Homestead may show a fall off in business in the past three months they attribute to Best Home's disparagement. They project that if this disparagement continues, it could put them out of business. Assuming that they can show a income statement that shows net profits at $10 million a year, the losses they may show would amount to approximately $100 million over ten years. The chances that they might get an injunction might be 5 percent, but, they might be will to spend $500,000 in litigation costs even if it is only a 5 percent chance of winning.

In a jury case, some attorneys also find it helpful knowing the latest percentages of plaintiff success once a case goes to a jury. For example, plaintiff's' lawyers quote a 70 percent win rate in front of Los Angeles County juries. Medical malpractice defense lawyers quote recent Center-for-State Courts statistics showing the doctors sued for malpractice win close to 60 percent of the time when the case goes to jury.[5] These percentages can again add information to a lawyer's case evaluation, so long as they realize the predictive nature of these figures and still assess the biasing factors of the individual case.

In a judge decider case, a particular judge may be known by his or her track record, to never give an injunction, and this may be useful in framing the prediction for the client.

Defendants' lawyers like to argue in negotiation, that economically speaking, the rational thing to do is weight each decision the jury needs to make by its probability of occurring in plaintiff's favor. So weighing duty, and weighing breach, proximate cause, and some damage would mathematically result in a better understanding of the probabilities involved. Instead of giving a probability to the chances of winning, they give a probability to each element of the cause of action, and multiply them together. For example, if proving a duty existed was 0.9, breach was 0.5, proximate cause was 0.7 and proving some damage was 0.9, then the probability of plaintiff success would be 0.2835.

Similarly, the chance of getting a preliminary injunction needs to be viewed in light of the court deciding Homestead's way on four different factors, the likelihood of success on the merits, the balance of harms, the adequate remedy at law, and on public policy issues of competition in the marketplace versus fair competition.

---

5. In fact, the centers statistics seemed to indicate that plaintiffs have a better chance to win if they try their case just to a judge.

Yet probability weighting could be more sophisticated, but less complicated. In the garden variety personal injury case, the plaintiff might argue that if breach is proven, then proximate cause and damages are virtual certainties. For example, in the personal injury example above, the probability might be .45 calculated by multiplying the percentage chance of prevailing on the issue of duty times the percentage chance of prevailing on breach. Plaintiffs would cite to attitudinal studies which seem to indicate that accountability for one's behavior is the Number One value in the United States today.[6] The jury would focus in on one tough decision concerning who is responsible—the blameworthiness of the defendant—and then simply do what was required after they made that decision.

Donald Vinson finds some support for plaintiffs' arguments[7] that jurors think deductively from certain strongly held values. This would mean that giving a single probability on liability may be more a more accurate predictor. For the purpose of early case evaluation, **focus groups** may provide the quickest and most accurate prediction of the attitudes jurors may have that are outcome determinative, and as a result best help the lawyer and client assess the cases chance of success before a jury. Pay $15 an hour to twelve persons whom you assemble that meet the demographics of your jury. Present opening statements on both sides, and for under $1,000 you can see where the jury is likely to come out. Of course, where the focus group has questions and proof can be obtained, you might refine your theories and themes in the process. In any event, for purposes of telling the client what the case is worth, the focus group could be a pretty good predictor of how the jury might respond to your case. Of course, the credibility of the witness will not be tested, but attitudinal values of the likely jurors could be surveyed to determine what the likely result would be.

Similarly, current thinking about preliminary injunctions suggests that balance of harms is the factor most heavily weighted in determining whether a preliminary injunction should be issued. Probability estimates that under-weighted this factor would not

---

6. For example, *Time* Magazine Poll, Spring 2000.

7. Donald E. Vinson, Jury Trials, *The Psychology of Winning Strategy*, 1-46.

provide the client with an accurate understanding of whether the client should seek an injunction.

In addition, early involvement of damages experts is important for case evaluation. Used as a consulting expert, as opposed to a testifying expert, such consultants can provide invaluable information for the client's valuation of the case and decision making. These experts provide great experience in helping the lawyer determine what variable may affect the damages figure, and the volatility of each variable. Armed with this information, the lawyer can better look for facts and evidence that will best fit what the expert needs to make the expert opinion reasonable and reliable.

Focus group results may also help the parties value their cases. Just as product marketers use focus groups to test market reactions to products and particular marketing strategies, focus groups can provide clients with better empirical evidence of what a case may be worth. If fairly and objectively presented, focus groups not only can give the parties insight into what themes will best resonate with jurors, but they can help the sides persuade each other that groups of likely juror place high or low values on an "objective" presentation of the case.

Finally, for the purpose of developing settlement authority from the client, there are three additional economic forces that need to be considered,

1. the expense already incurred and expense involved in further trial preparation, (while maybe not rational to consider, have a psychological affect on parties willingness to settle),

2. expense of the trial itself,

3. a discount factor until trial.[8]

Dealing with number 3 first, in some jurisdictions, trial could still be a long way off, and the further away it is the larger a big factor discounting may become. Moreover, if payment is going to be made over a significant period of time, as with structured payments,

---

8. This assumes you have already figured in the discount rate for determining the present value of future income streams. Of course, if your jurisdiction doesn't discount, and reasons that inflation and discount balance out, then don't discount.

then counsel needs to be familiar with the present-value-of-money calculations to advise the client about settlement authority.

In sum, an economic value of a case for developing client settlement authority would include total damages, subtraction of plaintiff fault, a weighing of this figure on percentage chance of winning and proving damages as predicted, any discounting for present value, and costs yet to be incurred in producing the result, minus lawyer's contingency fees or lawyers fees.

PDL (probability of defendant held liable)

multiplied by

TD (total expected damages)

multiplied by

P (probability of damages finding)

less

PPCN (probability of plaintiff's contributory negligence)

less

PPND (probability of plaintiffs damages associated with plaintiff's negligence)

less

D   (discount to present value)

less

C   (costs)

less

LF   (lawyer Fee)   =   **Case Value**

Using this formula can help prepare the lawyer for meetings with the client to discuss the legal and economic consequences of a decision, and will help the lawyer be more precise in informing the client in order to develop settlement authority. It will also help prepare the lawyer to be more persuasive during settlement negotiations.

5.2.2. **Client Role in Position Bargaining**

In this regard, we must turn to how the lawyer communicates this economic evaluation to the client. Of course, here is where the lawyer must be careful. In counseling the client, the plaintiff should be told how this figure depends on **persuading** the jury or decision maker about a number of key elements of the case, including duty, breach, proximate cause and damages. For example, the client needs to be told the jury may conclude future hospital treatment will cure the ailment (and for that reason reject alternative damages), or the jury may conclude another job will come along some where (and for that reason reject part of the damages calculation). Likewise), the jury may attribute only 30 percent of the total responsibility to the plaintiff if the court excludes evidence of plaintiff's drinking (because the Breathalyzer was under the legal limit), or if counsel is successful in keeping off the jury people who are religiously opposed to drinking.

Some lawyers like to summarize all the variables of prediction by giving a percentage chance of winning and **include** a **best possible alternative**, a **most likely alternative**, a **likely alternative**, and a **worst likely alternative**. In our example above, the lawyer might use these numbers: $2,880,000 as the best possible alternative; $2,016,000 as the most likely alternative; $100,000 as a likely alternative; and $0 as the worst alternative. The plaintiff might even weight these outcomes by percentage.

Best possible alternative	10 percent	$2,880,000
Most likely alternative	50 percent	$2,016,000
Likely alternative	30 percent	$100,000
worst likely alternative	10 percent	$0

In any event, the client is armed with substantially better information to make an informed decision, and the negotiator is more precise about what he thinks the case is worth and why.

Moreover, position bargainers argue that this kind of strategic thinking makes each side's thinking more objective and analytical. It better helps the bargainer "control" his own behavior during the negotiation, knowing the limits of his authority, and the steps he plans to take to arrive within a reasonable bottom line. In fact, each side's figures should not be that far apart. Often, experienced dispassionate business litigators prepare a valuation from the perspective of the opponent. Preparing from the opposing side's perspective better prepares the lawyer to anticipate the points of difference and prepare arguments to overcome those differences. This preparation process makes them better able to talk with each other and discover the strengths and weaknesses in each other's positions and reach a reasoned agreement. It is often the case that the lawyers work something out, even if on the court house steps, after jury **voir dire**, after opening statement, after closing argument and before the jury reaches a verdict, or the clients work something out in spite of their lawyers' failures to communicate. When this happens, the clients are guessing about outcomes, and assessing risks in the light of their views of their business objectives.

Recognize, however, that the rationality of the probability assigning process depends on the quality of the information each side has. Furthermore, the assignment of probabilities is an inherently value-laden process. Probabilities depend on experience, but experience is always seen through human eyes. So, where a CEO experiences law suits by the government, with eyes that see the market as having been harmed by excessive government regulation, the CEO may place a probability figure on the chances of a win based on the CEO's chances at doing something about a broader societal issue. Or the plaintiff (and attorney) may demonize the opponent and place probabilities on the outcome at court based on these biasing beliefs. Building in a range of probabilities can at times still provide an analytical basis for reasoned agreement.

Yet the position bargainer knows that he must plan to conduct the negotiation itself in order control the risks in any analytical approach to case valuation. He must test the other side's case to determine how good its information is, and whether the values of the opposing side so effect the valuation of the case, that his client is risking an unfair, disadvantageous resolution. The position bargainer sets up the negotiation, to help maximize its advantages concerning information exchange, bargaining positions and persuasion to move the opposition toward its view of the value of the case.

5.3 Planning for Position Bargaining

In the light of the foregoing discussion, consider how the strategic thinker would plan his litigation for a negotiated settlement.[9]

5.3.1 Step One: Information Exchange

The first step is to determine what style and strategy are most likely to produce the most information without revealing your own. Is it best to be friendly, creating a cooperative competition for information? Or is it better to be aggressively adversarial, and control and test information? Your thinking on this issue will help you plan whether and how to **select the forum**, conduct **ice breaking**, assert **agenda control**, employ appropriate **questioning strategies**, and prepare **blocks** that will help maximize an information exchange that will provide access to how the opposing side values their case, the opposing side's weaknesses, and any emotional or psychological factors that may effect case valuation.

5.3.2 Step Two: Response To Opening Offer

The negotiator needs to be careful not to "leak" too much information non-verbally when the opponent makes an offer. If he unintentionally reveals interest and acceptance, just like in a game of poker, he tips off the other side to what cards that they hold.

5.3.3 Step Three: Opening Offer

Prepare an opening offer that balances your credibility as a speaker with your position bargaining strategy of testing the other side's view of their and your case.

---

9. Guernsey and Zwier, *Advanced Negotiation and Mediation Theory and Practice: A Realistic Integrated Approach* (NITA, 2000.)

5.3.4 **Step Four: Persuasive Statements in Support of Your Positions**

Prepare a detailed, multifaceted, appropriately passionate presentation in support of your offer. Make it detailed, multifaceted, provide that it build, one argument on top of another, and prepare to deliver it with the right emotional fervor.

5.3.5 **Step Five: Plan Your Concessions**

Prepare ahead of time the timing, size, and decision factors that will give rise to concessions. Key is to prepare the size of the concession, because it can send signals as to where you have set the bottom line. Make sure to accompany each concession with a reason for your concession. Don't concede twice without your opponent conceding in between unless you initiate a second concession with a prior condition on the part of your opponent.

5.3.6 **Step Six: Test Your Opponents' Bottom Line**

Know the ethical parameters of persuasion in the context of negotiations. Much has been written about the ethical issues concerning the discussion in negotiation of the client's bottom line.[10] Recognize that if you ask your opponent, "Do you have authority to move off your last position?" you are putting them in a professional and tactical dilemma. If the opponent has room to move, and says no, he risks deadlock, and is in a conflict with the authority his client has given him. On the other hand, giving up client confidences about the client's communications to the lawyer about his bottom line is unethical.

5.3.6.1   **Ethical Parameters**

Some have argued that negotiators are free to lie if they are asked about their client's willingness to settle. Model Rule 3.4 and Comment 2 to Model Rule 4.1 seem to indicate as much. Take a look closely at Model Rules 3.4 and 4.1, and Comment 2 to 4.1.

---

10. See e.g. Charles B. Wiggins and L. Randolf Lowry, eds, *Negotiation and Settlement Advocacy, A book of Readings*, 2d ed. Chapter 16, (1997) (for 15 articles on the subject.)

MR 3.4 Fairness to Opposing Party and Counsel

A Lawyer shall not: falsify evidence, counsel or assist a witness to testify falsely, or offer an inducement to a witness that is prohibited by law.

MR 4.1 Truthfulness in Statements To Others

In the course of representing a client a lawyer shall not knowingly

a)   make a false statement of material fact or law to a third person: or

b)   fail fail to disclose a material fact to a person when disclosure is necessary to avoid assisting in a criminal or fraudulent act by a client, unless disclosure is prohibited by Rule 1.6.

Comment 2. Statements of Fact

[2] . . . Whether a particular statement should be regarded as one of fact can depend on the circumstances. Under the generally accepted **conventions** in negotiation, certain types of statements ordinarily are not taken as statements of material fact. **Estimates of price or value** placed on the subject of a transaction and a party's **intentions as to an acceptable settlement** or a claim are in this category, . . .

If you ask about your opponents' bottom line, or if they ask you about yours, you've created or are facing a dilemma. If you say you do not have authority to move, you may lock your self in at the expense of settlement. Consider each of the following options.

Based on what you have told me so far, I can't recommend that my client move off the earlier position.

You first! Can you move any more off of your earlier position?

I've been given broad discretion by my client, but I'm not willing to move, base on what I've learned so far.

Others try to manipulate the client's bottom line during a negotiation. They may counsel their client to give them only limited authority during the early stages of negotiation, so that they can use their client to slow down the bargaining process and get client input as more is learned about the other side's position.

5.3.7 **Prepare for Deadlock**

One of the problems with deadlock is that you must take the steps to prepare for trial, knowing that there might be other grounds of fruitful discussion that may lead to the resolution of the dispute. You should plan how to deal will deadlock. Will you walk out? Will you stay and bargaining hypothetically? Will you brainstorm with your opponent for creative ways to deal with the deadlock, taking the opportunity presented by the deadlock to bargain like problem solvers?

5.3.8 **Wrap Up**

Prepare to restate the terms of the agreement to be clear you have a deal on each issue that is important to your client.

5.3.9 **Write Up**

Plan ahead of time for who you will write up the deal. Save some emotional energy for the write up. Parties can add or try to subtract from what has been agreed to during the write up stage. Be careful here to not have celebrated too early, leaving yourself no reservoir of energy in case there are still problems with the deal.

5.4 **Problem Solving: A Second Approach**

As we have seen, dispute resolution theory and negotiation practice teaches that negotiation is not simply a matter of applying an objective economic analysis of case valuation and arriving at an answer. There is a psychology at work between agent bargainers, as well as between clients. To some, these psychological forces overwhelm the analytical ones, and make conflict resolution a fundamentally non-rational, if not irrational, process. They prefer position bargaining strategies to deal with social psychological issues. Others would rather use cooperative strategies to provide each side with a better understanding of the other's point of view. They argue that the conflict resolution process is dependent instead on building trust and building a relationship between the parties so that they choose to agree rather than fight.

Furthermore, the adversarial position bargaining strategies used by lawyers can exacerbate feelings of mistrust and competition. Some have argued that position bargaining also fails to produce creative, particularized and lasting solution between the parties.[11] They argue that a different strategy for negotiation is needed, one that makes joint problem solvers out of the negotiators in order that the parties will better resolve their dispute.

Let's look more closely at the psychology of each party in the decision making process to determine how to think differently, and strategically about the case.

Cognitive psychologists, especially the **behavioralists**, caution that even professional decision makers are not as rational as one might expect (especially as defined by optimal efficiency principles).[12] The parties might value their cases differently because one is more naïve and intuitive, or is susceptible to error or ideological bias. Or, one side's client or lawyer is just simply not very skilled at case valuation or counseling. They are stuck in the warrior mode, and miss the keys to case valuation and settlement.

---

11. Robert H. Mnookin, *Beyond Winning: Negotiation To Create Value in Deals and Disputes,* (Harvard University Press, 2000). Roger Fisher and William Ury, *Getting to Yes: Negotiating Agreement without Giving In* (NY Penguin Books, 1983).

12. Robert A. Prentice, *Chicago Man, K-T Man, and the Future of Behavioral Law and Economics,* 56 VAND. L. REV. 1663 (2003).

Professor Lagevoort, a social scientist who researches and analyzes disputes, describes cognitive psychological literature on decision making biases and advises lawyers to take interest in behavioral psychology as it affects decision making and may inhibit optimal conflict resolution.[13] This literature suggests that non rational biases come in seven forms.

NON RATIONAL BIASES

1. **Status quo/loss aversion biases and framing effects**	This bias is noted as a decision maker's preference for risk aversion and a natural bias for the status quo.
2. **Anchoring and adjustment**	People tend to "anchor" on some initial possibility in decision making, and fail to adjust carefully as new information becomes available.
3. **Illusory correlations and causation biases**	Clients often fined causal patterns and relationships in matters that are the product of random chance.
4. **Biases in risk perception**	Clients seem to ignore low risk factors that have not been made salient, or seem to value uncertainty differently at the extremes. For example studies suggest clients may ignore risk differences in gains in the 5 to 10 percent category, and place more significance on removing the 5 and less risk of a bad thing happening.
5. **The hindsight bias**	People overestimate their fault when they could have predicted the outcome, and the outcome happens.
6. **Context bias**	Relative preference between two outcomes may bias away from a compromise third outcome.
7. **Intertemporal biases**	There is a bias toward consumption and against deferred gratification.

Both lawyers and clients are affected by these biases. Lawyers then tend to think of negotiation as an opportunity to persuade the opposing party, not only as to the predicted value of the cases as a matter of economics, but also to "bias" the decision in their favor by persuading the other side as a matter of psychology. Focus

---

13. Donald C. Lagevoort, Symposium: *The Legal Implications of Psychology: Human Behavior, Behavioral Economics,* and the *Law: Behavioral Theories of judgment and Decision Making in Legal Scholarship.*

groups and mock trials can greatly aid in this process as they may provide the empirical correction necessary for the biasing effects on the various decision makers.

Lawyers who take a solely economic valuation view of negotiation—discovering expected values at trial, in the light of traditional court decisions—may run into two types of reactions from their opponents: their theory of negotiation ignores the social psychology inherent in dispute resolution, and can't account for the fact that courts, most often, are stuck with a win lose decision, while the parties themselves are not. In court, one party wins and one loses. A court is seldom able to customize a particularized solution to the parities' problem. Those solutions are left to the parties both before and after the court reaches its decision, and it is very difficult for a litigator not to think in win lose, "zero sum game" terms.

In addition, the negotiation process itself is fraught with additional psychological forces. Consider what we know from game theory.[14] Not only does competition produce its own psychological effect, but so do needs for **respect**, living up to **expectations** of others, feelings of **powerlessness, embarrassment or face saving, isolation**, views of **sunk costs** and **opportunity costs**, and **multicultural, gender,** and **ethnic differences** effect results in ways that make negotiation outcomes appear irrational. We would like to think that a professional experienced bargainer can factor out biases and psychological and social differences. The problem is that a lawyer is not immune to these same forces. In fact, watching pairs of lawyers negotiate in simulation settings, where one might expect less emotion, and less deadlock, what we have learned is that one of the major forces against reaching settlement, even where client authority overlaps and position bargaining ought to produce settlement, often the bargainers biases (for higher fees, even though purely hypothetical in the simulation) egos and anger block settlement.

5.5 Respect and Anger

One of the most difficult emotional forces at work that prevents conflict resolution, and, in fact, may escalate the conflict, is

---

14. Morton Deutsch and Peter T. Coleman, eds, *The Handbook of Conflict Resolution: Theory and Practice.*

anger. To see how this is so, think first about a conflict that arises between a parent and child, and how it informs our understanding of disputes, generally.

Imagine you are the parent of fifteen-year-old daughter. You, your wife, and other children are all waiting for the arrival of your fifteen-year-old daughter, so that you can leave on your long anticipated family vacation. You are making the trip by car, and need to leave at 4 P.M., to be able to stop for dinner and arrive at your cottage by 10 P.M. When your daughter left in morning for the last day of school, you made sure she knew to be home from school by 4 P.M. so that you could leave on time. Your last words to her were, "Don't be late." Now it is 4:30 P.M., and still no daughter. Your anger is rising.

Conflict resolution theorists tell us that what is likely to happen next is a problem inherent in coming together of anger and feelings of lack of respect.[15] What is likely is that you will attribute a motive to your daughter's lateness that may produce a significant long standing affect on your relationship with your daughter and you ability to resolve your conflict with her.

Imagine what might happen is you let your anger take over. You might yell at her for her behavior. You might attribute her behavior to lack of respect of you and the family. You might, without thinking, further attribute her behavior to a character defect she has, that she is inconsiderate, routinely late, and self centered. These and character traits you recognize because they come from you, (or her mother) and you were afraid they would surface in her, and now they have, and she has this flaw in her character.

She gets angry and cries. She says she was with her friends, and has a right to be! She says you are too compulsive, and what difference does it make if we get the cottage a few minutes later? She says that she is afraid of you, and that you can't control your temper, that she hates you and hates living in family. She runs into her room and slams the door.

What just happened is what conflict resolution theorists' describe as the volatile combination of attribution error and anger.

---

15. This is a scenario that is adapted from one used by Tom Rusk, *The Power of Ethical Persuasion*, 18–29, (1993)

Attribution is the process whereby the "harmdoer" and the harmed party assign responsibility for the harmdoer's behavior. Each confronts the other with a judgment about who is responsible for the harm. The judgment of responsibility turns on the nature of the harmdoer's excuses and motives for causing the harm. The judgment of appropriate responsibility can be laid out as follows:[16]

Intentional harmful behavior	leads to an apology, punishment, and the need to repay a fair amount.
Negligent harmful behavior	leads to a different kind of apology and a change in behavior over those things the harmdoer can fairly control, as well fair compensation.
Excusable harmful behavior	leads to no apology and no compensation.

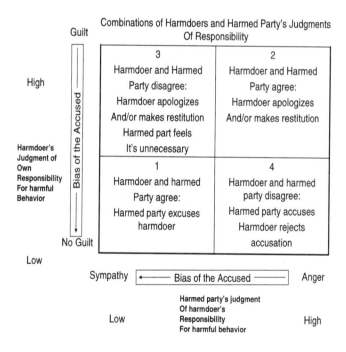

Of course, most of the time there is some combination of behavior or there is a disagreement about the nature of the excuses and whether they are controllable.

16. Keith G. Allred, Anger and Retaliation in Conflict, in Morton Deutsch and Peter T. Coleman, *Handbook of Conflict Resolution* 245, (2000).

Consider for example how differently you feel about the situation where what happened to your daughter was as follows: She was approached by a good friend in tears, who asked for her help. Her stepfather was approaching her sexually, and she wanted someone she knew to talk to. She did not know where to turn and wanted your daughter to talk to her and help her figure out what best to do. A paradigm shift has just occurred.[17] It is inappropriate for you to have been angry, because you daughter's excuse relates to circumstances beyond her control. You would have been disappointed in her if she had not taken the time to talk to her friend. You might have preferred for her to have called and explained the situation, but still you do not blame her, nor is it fair to attribute responsibility to her that would require the same level of apology, punishment, and compensation that you and she might otherwise feel is appropriate.

Moreover, there is more at stake here. Because of your anger, you have attributed her behavior to disrespectful at best, self centeredness, and more likely, an intentional motive to harm the family. These attribution errors can cause the most damage to the ability of the parties to resolve the conflict. If the parties are not able to fairly assess what excuses are in actuality available, and whether they are beyond the control of the harmdoer, the parties are likely to attribute the behavior to intent, disrespect, and character flaws, provoking not guilt, but a righteous sense of being wronged, harmed, and unfairly blamed. These feeling will likely provoke an escalating response, of the kind you gave in your anger.

How often does a lawyer get angry during a negotiation? How often is that anger a result of the lawyer perceiving that the opponent does not respect either the lawyer or lawyer's client? They attribute the behavior of their opponent and or opponent's representative to an intention to harm, or to a character flaw in the opponent or client, or industry they represent. When anger occurs, the negotiators tend to say things that attribute the worst motives to their opposition and that are destructive of resolving disputes. They attribute greed and disrespect to the harmdoer or to the harmed party. Their lawyers tend to exaggerate the dispute

---

17. Steven Covey, *Seven Habits of Highly Effective People*, "Habit 5," (where Covey argues that effective people should try not to react in anger, but seek first to understand, before being understood. He otherwise refers to this habit as the habit of "courageous compassion." See, Stephen R. Covey *Principled-Centered Leadership*, 45, 1992)

by taking extreme positions. Then their opponents can point to these exaggerations as evidence of their opponent's lying. As a result they justify tactics that obfuscate, deny responsibility, and justify taking further extreme positions because of the fear that any admission will be used to unfairly punish and exact retribution. Conflict escalates and can lead to deadlock, unless cooler heads prevail.

What does it mean in this context for cooler heads to prevail? The lawyer must think strategically for ways to deal with his or her own anger, and think strategically for ways to deal with the opponent's anger. The first problem is one that is related to self control, and can be managed very much like any self control issue. Like an addiction, the problem with anger is that, to some, it feels good, it is born of an instinct to fight, is related to adrenalin, and feelings of power, and for some, is very hard to control. For the lawyer, it is often confused with the legitimate role that the lawyer must play, to passionately and zealously represent their clients within the bounds of law.

Because our opponents may be cowered by anger and "flee" rather than fight, if they think the anger is irrational enough, the effect may be that the negotiator's anger produces the desired effect, an outcome in his client's favor. After all, for a threat to be effective, it must be heard, understood, and believed. The emotion and passion of the speaker communicates a willingness to back up their position with violence, if necessary, and, at times, aids in the "believability" part of making a threat effective.

At risk, however, are escalation, deadlock, and permanent damage to the relationship. Interestingly, expressing a position in anger may make one more wedded to it and less willing to see the weakness in the position. In addition, a skilled opponent may see anger as weakness, not strength, and related to the flight instinct. The opponent may also see the failure of self control as a character flaw, indicating lack of confidence in the client's position. The lawyer needs to be able to understand anger and manage it in order to implement the client's goals.

5.6 **Anger Management**

First, the lawyer must recognize that he is feeling angry and the reactive effect on his behavior. With this self knowledge in hand the lawyer can plan what to do if the feeling of anger arises; including using role plays and developing habits, to better control the anger. Some suggest that an effective way to manage anger is to develop a self-regulatory plan and implementation strategy. Just as a smoker who is trying to quit might plan for what to do when he or she craves a smoke, the lawyer might plan for when he starts to feel angry. The more specific the plan, the better your chances of overcoming the feeling.

For example, a lawyer might plan as follows:

1. When the lawyer accuses me of being unreasonable in my demand for damages, I will cite specific recent decisions and settlements of similar size.

2. I will say to myself, this little mantra, "Do not get angry. Anger is not helpful, and will harm the client."

3. If the opponent rejects those cases and refuses to discuss them because my client was negligent, recognize the tactic as a position bargaining tactic, and not a personal affront. Plan, instead, to ask the opponent to place probabilities on the jury so finding, and if the opponent refuses, plan to write down your own probability, in order to keep yourself more analytical, and less emotional.

Anger management has steps. It involves recognition of the feeling, and the development of a mantra. It often gives the person something physical to do; like writing down what you will do next, or writing what you will say before you say it, or playing with a piece of tape. In addition it provides for a backup. In other words, when the feelings are very powerful, give yourself someplace to

go, take a break or something else to talk about, or someone else
to talk to or involve in the process.[18]

When the negotiator sees anger in his opponent, the negotiator can also plan for what to do. Naming it (saying that your
opponent is angry) and taking a time out are common effective
strategies. Examining your own behavior to determine whether
you might have unfairly caused the anger, and apologizing, is also
a very good place to start.[19]

Experiences with adversarial bargaining have caused conflict
resolution theorists to yearn for a better model for conducting negotiations resolving conflicts.

A **problem-solving** model seeks to create a set of negotiating
steps and procedures that will better control against the biasing effects on client decision-making, and better control the social and
psychological forces that lead to deadlock. It also tries to create
a different more creative strategy to devise more particularized
creative solutions.

Problem solving attempts to learn from psychiatry. Psychia-
trists recommend that counselors, negotiators, and mediators
seek to listen for understanding before attempting to persuade, in
order to keep the emotions from biasing the decision making.[20] In
order to resist the adversarial role-playing involved in most position bargaining, the problem solver should initially serve the role
as "listener."[21] The need for true understanding is a threshold for

---

18. Walter Mishel and Aaron L. DeSmet, *Self-Regulation in the Service of Conflict
Resolution*, in Morton Deutsch and Peter T. Coleman, *The Handbook of Conflict Resolution*, 269–270, (2000).

19. Kieth G. Allred, Anger and Retaliation in Conflict, in Morton Deutsch and Peter T.
Coleman, *The Handbook of Conflict Resolution*, 246 (2000).

20. Tom Rusk, M.D., with D. Patrick Miller, *The Power of Ethical Persuasion*, 68–69,
(1993).

21. The role of "listener" in litigation work was introduced by Maude Pervere and Janeen Kerper at a planning conference held by the National Institute for Trial Advocacy
(NITA) for developing of a new program for lawyers to examine the lawyer client relationship. Pervere and Kerper then referred us to Tom Rusk's work, *The Power of Ethical
Persuasion* (1993) (Hereinafter Rusk). Rusk is a noted psychiatrist who has been instru-
mental in developing models for teaching community mediation

any connectedness and necessary empathy and is best described in the work of psychiatrist Tom Rusk.[22] He writes,

> It's mysterious and ironic that after millions of years of evolution—and a hundred or so of modern psychological theorizing and research—we humans have not advanced very far in person-to-person communications. We can generally exchange thoughts and ideas pretty well, but nonetheless we often fail to *understand* each other. For the most part, what we fail to communicate clearly is our feelings, those nonverbal, deeply rooted energies that can lead us to act in contradiction to our will and our rational decisions. Between people, strong feelings can easily escalate a simple misunderstanding into a senseless battle of wills. Even wars between nations have begun that way.
>
> Modern psychology has done relatively little to help us comprehend our feelings, or learn to manage them in *understanding, caring,* and *fairness* in order to create happier, more fulfilling lives. (Emphasis in the original.) Many successful books on communication strategies have sought to teach people how to expedite problem solving or gain the upper hand in all kinds of negotiations. But these strategies almost always ignore the power of feelings in all kinds of relationships, and the need to uphold explicit social values in the conduct of human communication.
>
> As far as I'm concerned, there never was or will be a better basic communication strategy than the Golden Rule: *Do unto others as you would have them do unto you.* Ethical persuasion is a practical, strategic method of applying the Golden Rule to every kind

---

22. *The Power of Ethical Persuasion.* Rusk's listening techniques correspond with the techniques that Mnookin describes in his book, *Beyond Winning: Negotiation to Create Value in Deals and Disputes,* and Fisher and Ury describe in their book, Getting to Yes. Rusk's listening techniques in *The Power of Ethical Persuasion* correspond with the techniques that Mnookin describes in his book, *Beyond Winning: Negotiation to Create Value in Deals and Disputes,* and Fisher and Ury describe in their book, *Getting to Yes* (NY: Penguin Books, 1983).

of important communication—not as a means of
merely doing a "good deed," but as a means of giving everyone a fair hearing, creating the optimal solutions for thorny problems, and fostering long term,
trusting relationships.

Rusk's ethical persuasion is the practical "how to" for the moral philosophy of persuasion. Rusk describes seven steps to good
listening.

1. Establish that your immediate goal is mutual understanding, not problem solving.

2. Elicit the other person's thoughts, feelings, and
   desires about the subject at hand.

3. Ask for the other person's help in understanding
   him or her. Try not to defend or disagree.

4. Repeat the other person's position in your own
   words to show you understand.

5. Ask the other person to and keep restating his or
   her position.

6. Refer back to your position only to keep things
   going.

7. Repeat steps 1–6 until the other person unreservedly agrees that you understand his or her
   position.[23]

5.7 Listening Is A Key

Listening, then, is a key to understanding, and understanding
is key to solving problems within the moral orientation that takes
feelings into account, but does not provide them with unfair, or bias
infect. Listening should be done first because it will help break the
lawyer out of the position bargaining role playing. It establishes the
lawyer in the learning mode first, as opposed to the doing mode.

---

23. Rusk, supra, note 53, at 7–8.

It subverts what the lawyer knows to what the opponent knows and feels. In addition, to the extent that information is power, the listener has the advantage of knowing both sides (the lawyer's and the opponent's) before speaking. In addition, listening earns the listener the leverage of fairness. The more the opponent is listened to and understood, the more the opponent will likely listen and seek understanding in return. Finally, these seven steps cultivate in the listener's patience and openness, which are behaviors that evidence respect.[24]

Again, Rusk has some concrete practical advice for the negotiator during the third step where the lawyer may express his position in the matter. Rusk's concrete steps better ensure that the advocate is acting out of the perspective of respect. Rusk describes these as follows:[25]

1. Ask for a fair hearing in return.

2. Begin with an explanation of how the other person's thoughts and feelings affect you. Avoid blaming and self-defense as much as possible.

3. Carefully explain your thoughts, desires, and feelings as your truth, not the truth.

4. Ask for restatements of your position—and corrections of any factual inaccuracies—as necessary.

5. Review your respective positions.

The result is that the win/lose, "I'm right and you're wrong," dichotomy may immediately be broken. The possible solutions that arise multiply greatly when the focus turns to what will create, maintain or maximize the healthy relationships already present in the situation. Within a relationship of trust and respect, each negotiator will look for ways for each side to win.

Ask yourself what difference it makes if, instead of asking, "Can we win an injunction?" the lawyer asks himself, "Are there any alternatives where everyone can win? You might ask

---

24. Id. at 69–70.
25. Id. At 89.

the client different types of questions with a problem solving
strategy in mind. For example, you might ask,

What is the market conflict?

Do people who can afford Homestead Housing,
qualify for financing for Best Homes?

Are you really competitors?

Could you agree to refer customers to each other?

Can Homestead help Best Homes build better
cheaper stand alone homes by using the mass
manufacturing process?

Within a relationship of trust and respect between bargainers,
it is more likely that bargainers may think in these terms. It is also
more likely that the lawyers will prepare by asking their client's
the tough questions.

What was said about the quality of Homestead's
homes?

What is the quality control procedures Homestead uses to insure product design and installa-
tion quality?

What information did Best Homes have about the
quality of Homestead's homes?

What is fair for each to contribute for the fair resolution of what was said?

Depending on the answers to these questions the problem solving negotiators and their clients can cut through the adversarial
rights based analysis and frame a quicker and better solution.

To get into this problem-solving mind set is not easy. Problem
solvers advise that their model works best when both negotiators
have agreed to such a strategy. They suggest opening statements
carefully designed to try to get buy in from the opposing negotiator

for taking a more open and problem solving approach. If, however, the other side has taken a hard bargaining approach—extreme positions, followed by small concessions, with little analytical support for the positions taken—it does not mean that by careful planning and taking a problem solving lead, by example, that problem solving can not occur.

1. Plan for setting the right tone

2. Make your process explicit and include your view of the benefits of a problem solving approach

3. Describe underlying needs and goals of each side, and seek information about the needs and goals of the other side

4. Use active listening and ethical persuasion techniques to build trust

5. Use analytical structures to try and give rise to a valuation that will be able to with stand a fairness critique

5.8 Negotiation Strategy and Client Counseling

Formulating and implementing a problem solving negotiation strategy is integrally connected to client counseling. If you have chosen a problem-solving approach you may have a challenging educational process on your hands regarding the client. To be the most effective problem solver you need the client to buy into taking a more creative problem-solving approach to try to reach an early settlement. You will need a more detailed and complete understanding of the client's goals and values. The better the lawyer understands the client, the better the lawyer will be able to determine a value for the case: the bottom lines for both parties, and build strategies for building trust and relationships between the parties. Also, the better the lawyer understands the client's goals and values, the better the lawyer can search for a more particularized problem-solving solution.[26]

---

26. Mnookin, *Beyond Winning*, chapter 7 (2000).

Still, in the real world of lawyer negotiation, despite the careful planning of the negotiator, the opposition may not want to play. He may use the apparent cooperative setting to block giving truthful information, and discover the weaknesses in your case, without any trade of information and understanding of the weaknesses in his own case. Some even argue, that as in the international arena, it is ineffective if not unethical for a bargainer to worry about anything but his client's (nations) own interests. Some considerations are that position bargaining strategies are a matter of human nature (inherent selfishness): that human nature dictates behavior, that in the end, requires the negotiator to be suspicious of and mistrust his opponents, and see any attempt to be open and cooperate as a manipulative strategy designed to give his opponent undue leverage in the resolution of the dispute.

In any event, it is true that lawyers need to be cautious in implementing problem solving models when their opponents may not be bargaining in good faith. It is important to realize, however, the advantages of cooperative problem solving in order to advice the client about the potential use of a mediator. Moreover, the lawyer needs to understand these two different strategies and approaches to negotiation—both position bargaining and problem solving, in order to plan and advise the client about the potential strategic uses of a mediator to help resolve the dispute.

5.9 Mediation In The context of A Position-Bargaining Strategy

Mediators provide a number of useful purposes when seen in the light of a position bargaining strategy.

- The mediator can lend credibility to the client's valuation of the case

- The mediator can help the parties get information about the opponent's bottom line, strengths and weaknesses in their case

- The mediator can act as an expert evaluator of the case in light of the experience in judging responsibility or evaluating credibility and persuasiveness of stories, and in light their substantive/technical expertise

- The mediator can use position bargaining strategies to move the parties to a reasoned settlement

- Use of deadlines

- Probe positions and test them for evidence

- Use of contracts and processes for exchange of information

- Use of confidentiality and caucuses to "leak" information to each side

- Use of persuasion

- Use of trading concessions of equal value

- Splitting the difference

5.10 Mediation In The Context of A Problem-Solving Strategy

Some mediators, thought of as neutral facilitators, eschew valuation and position bargaining strategies when they conduct mediations. Facilitative mediators are particularly good for implementation of a problem solving strategy for resolving the dispute. If the mediator will use techniques to maintain neutrality, refuse case evaluation, facilitate communication, and use brainstorming and other counseling techniques to create win/win solutions, then the mediator can be vital to the implementation of a problem solving strategy.

The problem-solving mediator can:

- Suggest problem solving processes

- The mediator can overcome opponent resistance to problem solving strategies by making suggestions from the position of neutrality. Where these same solutions suggested by a lawyer negotiator might be rejected because they are distrusted and viewed as tricks and manipulations, when offered by a neutral they will more likely be adopted

- Facilitate discussion of underlying goals and values

- Create fair processes for providing information and valuation

- Facilitate the generation of multiple alternative solutions that create win-win outcomes

- Suggest creative valuation methods to provide means for parties to turn values into positions

- Create implementation processes that build fairness, predictability, and trust

5.11 Problem-Solving Mediation Will Affect Advocacy Strategy.[27]

Where a mediator is a problem solver/neutral, the mediator may structure and control the mediation to discourage position bargaining. So, a mediator may forbid opening offers. The mediator may refuse to evaluate either the facts or the legal outcome. The mediator may discourage individual caucuses with either side or lawyer in order to keep the parties hearing and trusting each other, and not sowing distrust of the mediator, by engaging in confidential communications with one side or the other.

This structure affects a number of advocacy strategies in mediation, including an understanding that opening statements are not directed to the mediator, but directed to the opposing party. The opening might describe the history of the dispute, but not detail positions, favoring instead statements of broad goals and interests, to arm the negotiator to facilitate creative problems solving.

In addition to affecting the substance of what the advocate presents, a problem-solving mediation will affect the advocates tone, language, and structure of presentation. In addition, the advocate will be suggesting ways the mediator can facilitate resolution of the dispute. This requires an analysis of the type of dispute,

---

27. Hal Abrahmson, *Mediation Representation: Advocating In A Problem-Solving Process* (NITA 2004).

(whether the dispute is about data (proof), principle, a need for vindication, or is a matter of a misunderstanding or problem in communication.) Each type of dispute will require different mediation tools, and the advocate must realize that how these disputes are framed or characterized can greatly affect the outcome.

5.12 Application To *Homestead*

In order to understand this point the lawyer needs to think about how a mediator might facilitate a different kind of resolution of the dispute between Homestead and Best Homes. To Homestead, in problem I, focusing on broader client goals and objectives might lead the lawyer to recommend and the client to choose mediation.

The Homestead client might have the following, somewhat conflicting goals and objectives stated as follows:

- The client wants an injunction, and wants any damages to its reputation and sales that have resulted and will result from Best Homes conduct.

- The client wants to compete fairly in the market place, and wants Best Homes to stop unfairly competing by telling lies about the client to consumers.

- The client wants to do business without needlessly and inefficiently litigating which will raise the costs and create animosity that late may further damage Homestead's place in the market place.

Whereby employing a classic position bargaining strategy, it is unlikely that the parties will think to come armed with the information to engage in broader problem solving. Even if the parties tried to implement a problem solving strategy in the negotiation, without buy in up front, the early sessions are likely to be unproductive, until the bargainer is prepared on a broader understanding of the client's goals, or, in the worst case, feign interest in problem solving, only to discover weaknesses in Homestead's case.

Suggesting a facilitative mediator creates a different incentive. Parties will likely be required to be present. The mediator can ask critical questions of each side, and brainstorm for various alternatives. Other broader business concerns might be explored, and agreements might be reached which helped the parties fairly work together to promote each side's legitimate interests. (Of course this raises interesting anti-competitive possibilities that the lawyers may advise are illegal, but a knowledgeable mediator should know how to steer clear of illegal solutions.)

5.13 Intractable Conflicts

In the business context in particular, where a client may more readily think in terms of transactions, rather than disputes, these mediator facilitated problem solving solution might often work to the overall betterment of both sides. Other times, however, the parties are not able to negotiate unassisted to an agreement. Perhaps there is bad blood between the clients, or their lawyers, or there is too much at stake, or it is a matter of principal. Peter Coleman, Director of the International Center for Cooperation and Conflict Resolution, sheds light on intractability of conflicts in traditional litigation.[28]

1. **Time and intensity.** His first factor of intractability is the time and intensity of the conflict. It is interesting to note how the process of complaint and answer, interrogatories and depositions add time and intensity in the dispute between the parties and certainly to their lawyers.

2. **Issue centrality.** The second factor is issue centrality: that the conflict involves needs or values that the disputants experience as critical to their own survival.

3. **Conflict pervasiveness.** Third is conflict pervasiveness: that the conflict affects the disputants in their everyday life and work.

4. **Hopelessness**. Next is a feeling the parties share, that feeling is one of hopelessness.

---

28. Peter T. Coleman, *Intractable Conflict,* 428, in Morton Duetch and Peter T. Coleman, *Handboook of Conflict Resolution,* 428, (2000).

5. **Motivated to harm.** Fifth, parties are motivated to harm the other side. In the litigation process, the parties have sought Rule 11 sanctions, made ethics complaints to the bar about the lawyers, and have stated intentions to "destroy," "put out of business," and "make sure that this never happens again."

6. **Resisted efforts to resolve.** Finally, the parties have repeatedly resisted efforts to resolve the dispute, but nothing seems to have worked. Here is where the lawyer most often may see the need for mediation; where he has been involved in protracted and heated negotiations, with no movement between the parties.[29]

Again, however the social science literature suggests how mediators might help resolve even intractable conflicts. Peter Coleman suggests a number of guidelines that should be employed to try and overcome the resistance the parties have to settlement.

Guideline 1

Conduct a thorough analysis of the conflict system (its history, context, issues, and dynamics) prior to intervention

Here is where mediators can design a presentation process in the hearing of the concerned parties to make sure each side gets a chance to be heard, and be assured that the mediator understands the perspective of each party. Rusk's listening for understanding model is particularly good for fulfilling this guideline.

Guideline 2

Initial concern for the mediator should be to establish or foster an authentic experience of "ripeness" among the disputants or among the key representatives of each of the groups.

---

29. Peter T. Coleman and Morton Deutsch, *The Handbook of Conflict Resolution, Theory and Practice,* Chapter 21, p. 429–439, (2000)

Lawyers can help create this sense of ripeness by picking a skilled and fair mediator who has been successful in other difficult disputes and helps create a just and particularized solution to the dispute that lasts. The reputation of the mediator can create a sense of "ripeness" among the parties that now is the time to get this settled. One variable that can help the lawyer in suggesting the timing of the mediation can be whether there has been a recent or near catastrophe. In addition, if the cost of stalemate has been recalculated and is now projected to raise unacceptable costs to both sides (for example, the likely number of plaintiffs in future class will make it such that existing plaintiffs will not receive fair compensation) then the time is ripe for mediation.

Guideline 3

Initially, the mediator should orient the disputants toward the primary objective of defining a fair, constructive process of conflict engagement, and away from the objectives of achieving outcomes that resolve the conflict.

Before resolving the conflict the parties should focus on a fair process. This required input from the harmed and flexibility from the mediator, to hear the objections, and help design a process that would be fair. Again, a skilled mediator is vital to this occurring, but lawyers can "feed" the mediator suggestions regarding a fair process that will live within the limits of the client's goals and objectives.

Guideline 4

Given the complexity of intractable conflict, analysis and intervention must be embedded in a multidisciplinary framework.

Where a lawyer understands the social, psychological, economic, and justice implications involved in an intractable dispute, he can best prepare a process that will satisfy the parties. For example, where there are multiple parties in a mass tort setting and multiple interests, democratic theories require that each party has representation and a voice in the design of the process. In addition, any economic analysis needs to be designed to insure a reliable process of valuing individual harms. Document retrievals and language searches need to be designed that will insure fairness. Experts need to be drawn from different disciplines to advise and provide balance for different biases with in fields. The process needs to open. The steps in each decision need to be clearly articulated. Panels of decision makers must be accountable for their decisions. While mediators can design these, again the lawyers and their clients can suggest structure that works and lasts.

Guideline 5

Elicitive approaches to conflict intervention, particularly when working across cultures, tend to be more respectful of disputants, more empowering and sustainable, and generally more effective than prescriptive approaches.

The problem solvers and facilitative neutral mediators are cheering! Back by theories of representative democracy, these mediators attempt to get the disputants to suggest the solutions, arguing that they are more likely to own it and abide by it than if it is forced on them. These studies suggest that what is true about democratic representative processes on a national or international scale is true in private litigation. If the disputants can suggest, have input, and seem to have selected the process, they are more likely to live by it. Again, the litigator might suggest that the mediator propose a solution to the other disputants and see if they can see it as their own demand, that the litigant is "forced" to accede to.

Guideline 6

Short term (crisis management) interventions need to be coordinated and mindful of long term objectives and intervention.

This guideline is for the mediator, but it is the job of the advocate to remind the mediator of the long term goals of his client in mediation, and insure that these goals are not harmed.

Guideline 7

When working with conflicts between large groups (such as ethnic groups and communities), it is useful to concentrate interventions on the "mid-level" leadership representing each group.

Coleman writes about this guideline in the context of international disputes:

The work of John Burton, Herbert Kelman, John Paul Lederach, and others have emphasized targeting for intervention certain types of leader with groups and communities engaged in protracted social conflicts. These leaders, labeled "track II diplomats" or "middle-range leaders," are typically influential, unofficial representatives (members of the media; former or potential government officials; leaders of business, educational, religious, union, and other local institutions) from opposing sides of a conflict who represent the mainstream of each community and reflect the attitudes and interests of their respective communities.

There are several advantages to working with such [a mid-level]. It is efficient because mid-level representatives have influence going up and down the ladder. Mid-level representatives are more realistic because these have seen the good and bad in the parties they represent. They are also not usually constrained by their roles to take the more extreme positions.

A lawyer might suggest that a different cast of characters be present at a mediation session. The lawyer might look for mid level line workers as sources of both apologies, and or to build consensus about what is the realistic and fair thing to do to resolve a dispute.

Guideline 8

The general intervention strategy must integrate appropriate approaches for issues rooted in the past, the present, and the future.

Mediators mediating the mass multiparty dispute are worried that any short-term solution will be short term and leave future claimants without a remedy. Again, the litigator should prepare for the mediation ready to show why the resolution is designed to last.

Mediators mediating the mass multiparty dispute worry that any short term solution will be short term and leave future claimants without a remedy. Again, the litigator should prepare for the mediation ready to show why the resolution is designed to last.

For a litigator to think strategically about implementing the client's goals and objectives, the litigator needs to understand theory choices and strategies that are likely to come into play. The two prominent strategies are position bargaining, or adversarial bargaining, and problem solving. Position bargaining is the most common strategy employed by bargainers and involves taking positions to learn how your opponent likely sees his case and to determine how to move the opposition into a solution that meets your client's goals. Problems solving, on other hand, involves creating a relationship between the parties of trust and cooperation, in order that better and more creative solution can be devised. Problem solving strategies often require the involvement of a mediator, so the promise of problem solving be fully implemented.

Understanding these strategy choices can help you better counsel the client about the means by which his goals might be achieved. The strategies can also be useful for helping both client and lawyer understand the strengths, weaknesses, and risks involved in resolving their case, and finally, help the client best make the strategic moves to implement his goals.

❬•❭ ❬•❭ ❬•❭

FURTHER READING

Books

Peter T. Coleman and Morton Deutsch, *The Handbook of Conflict Resolution, Theory and Practice* (2000).

Harold Abramson, *Mediation Representation: Advocating In A Problem-Solving Process* (NITA 2004).

Bastrass, R. & Harbaugh, J., *Interviewing, Counseling, and Negotiating* (1990).

John W. Cooley, *Mediation Advocacy* 2d ed. (NITA, 2002).

Roger Fisher and William Ury, *Getting to Yes* (NY: Penguin, 1983).

Thomas F. Guernsey and Paul J. Zwier, *Advanced Negotiation and Mediation Theory and Practice,* (NITA, forthcoming in 2005).

Robert H. Mnookin, *Beyond Winning,* (Harvard Press 2000).

Gerald R. Williams, *Handbook on Effectiveness in Legal Negotiation: A System for Maximizing Negotiator Effectiveness* (1977).

Articles

Articles found in Charles B. Wiggins and L. Randolph Lowry, eds. *Negotiation and Settlement Advocacy: A Book of Readings* (2005)